Cincinnati's Lost Architects
Joseph and Bernard Steinkamp

THOMAS H. CONNOR

Copyright © 2021 by Thomas H. Connor. All rights reserved.

This book or any portion thereof may not be reproduced or used in any manner whatsoever without the express written permission of the publisher except for the use of brief quotations in a scholarly work or book review. For permissions or further information contact Braughler Books LLC at:

   info@braughlerbooks.com

Cover photos: Xavier campus. Xavier University. Used with permission
American Building. http://www.cincinnativiews.net/

Printed in the United States of America
Published by Braughler Books LLC., Springboro, Ohio

First printing, 2021

ISBN: 978-1-970063-98-1

Library of Congress Control Number: 2021919692

Ordering information: Special discounts are available on quantity purchases by bookstores, corporations, associations, and others. For details, contact the publisher at:

   sales@braughlerbooks.com

   or at 937-58-BOOKS

For questions or comments about this book, please write to:

   info@braughlerbooks.com

Dedication

To Emily who kept me company while I was writing this book.

Contents

Prologue vii

CHAPTER 1 Introduction: Steinkamp Family and Professional Activity 1

CHAPTER 2 Downtown Cincinnati 15

CHAPTER 3 Xavier University Campus 47

CHAPTER 4 Avondale and North Avondale 55

CHAPTER 5 Walnut Hills and East Walnut Hills 65

CHAPTER 6 Clifton, Corryville, and Mt. Auburn 81

CHAPTER 7 Price Hill, Delhi, Westwood, and South Fairmont 95

CHAPTER 8 St. Bernard 123

CHAPTER 9 Hyde Park 129

CHAPTER 10 Evanston 135

CHAPTER 11 Anderson and Mariemont 141

CHAPTER 12 Other Ohio Cities 145

CHAPTER 13 Works Outside Ohio 155

CHAPTER 14 Patents of Joseph G. Steinkamp 159

References 163

Index 195

Acknowledgments 207

About the Author 209

Prologue

FOR THE STRVCTVRE THAT WE RAISE,
TIME IS WITH MATERIALS FILLED;
OVR TO-DAYS AND YESTERDAYS
ARE THE BLOCKS WITH WHICH WE BVILD.
—Henry Wadsworth Longfellow, *By the Fireside*

Inscription on the fireplace at
Joseph G. Steinkamp's residence
at 916 Suire Avenue,
Price Hill, Ohio (ca. 1928)

When one thinks of late 19th or early 20th century architecture in Cincinnati, Ohio, one inevitably thinks of Samuel Hannaford and, later, Samuel Hannaford and Sons, the most prolific architectural firm in Cincinnati during this era. Samuel Hannaford is credited with designing Cincinnati City Hall, the Music Center, the Cincinnati Observatory, and many other notable buildings in and around the city. Or, one may think of James W. McLaughlin, considered the most original local architect of his generation. However, a German-American architect, Joseph G. Steinkamp, and his brother, Bernard F. Steinkamp, were major contributors to the architectural landscape of downtown Cincinnati and many of its suburbs. The firm, known as *Joseph G. Steinkamp and Bro., Architects and Superintendents*, was responsible for many different types of structures in the Cincinnati area that are still evident today.

The Steinkamp designs include distinctive private homes, flats, row houses, large apartment buildings, schools, churches, banks, theaters, and high-rise structures. In addition to three of their more prominent buildings in downtown Cincinnati—the American Building, the Mercantile Library, and the Hotel Metropole (now the 21c Hotel)—they designed the earliest buildings on the Xavier University campus. Many of their fine buildings are still standing today, although many others have been demolished and replaced with new buildings. As the city began to grow beyond the confines of the downtown area, their work spread with it, climbing the surrounding hills along with the emerging street cars.

Often partnering with the firm of *Thomas Emery's Sons*, the Steinkamps contributed to many large apartment buildings in downtown Cincinnati, Walnut Hills, Clifton, Avondale, and other areas. Many of these have been updated and modernized and are still in use today. However, their work also took them outside Cincinnati and included buildings in Dayton, Oxford, and Fayetteville in Ohio, and even into Kentucky, Indiana, and West Virginia.

In 1928, Joseph built a unique home for himself and his family in Price Hill that contained many distinctive features. In addition to the large limestone fireplace with the Longfellow quote, the living room and dining room had cathedral ceilings with ornately stenciled beams, large wrought iron and brass chandeliers, intricate terrazzo floors, and leaded glass windows with whimsical figures etched in them. Among the other features are a beautiful depiction of the Steinkamp coat-of-arms at the peak of the living room and three carved "envy heads" outside the master bedroom. Unfortunately, for reasons unknown, he lived in this home for only just over one year before it was sold at auction.

When I purchased his home in 2003, I learned some of its history and facts about Joseph and his brother, Bernard. As I started to delve into their history, I quickly learned how prodigious the brothers were, designing close to 300 structures in and around Cincinnati. I would guess that there are quite a few more of their works out there that I was not able to locate. This led me on a quest that inspired the writing of this book. Along the way, I have learned a considerable amount about Cincinnati history and have gotten to meet several of Joseph and Bernard's descendants and been helped by many generous people who have provided me with valuable information. Although I have striven to be as accurate as possible, I am sure I have made some mistakes long the way. It was not uncommon to find names misspelled, addresses or years stated incorrectly, and other inconsistencies. I have tried to identify at least two pieces of information for each building but sometimes that was not possible. I hope that you will enjoy reading about their story as much as I did uncovering it.

CHAPTER 1

Introduction: Steinkamp Family and Professional Activity

The end of the 19th century and the beginning of the 20th century were exciting yet unsettling times in Cincinnati and for the country. In 1893, Nikola Tesla and others were amazing the visitors at the World Columbian Exposition in nearby Chicago with the power of alternating current.[1] However, this period also brought a national economic crisis created by the collapse of the Philadelphia and Reading Railroad and the National Cordage Company.[2] Nevertheless, Cincinnati put on a grand celebration with the Centennial Exposition of the Ohio Valley and Central States in 1888.[3]

By 1890, Cincinnati, the largest city in Ohio, had become an important industrial, political, literary, and educational center in both Ohio and the United States. More than 15 railroads connected Cincinnati to other parts of the country. The major industries in Cincinnati were iron production, meatpacking, cloth production, and woodworking. Cincinnati had about 130 newspapers and magazines, and the University of Cincinnati provided residents with access to a college education. At the turn of the new century, the city was served by five hospitals and more than 200 churches.[4]

At this time in Cincinnati, architect *Johann B. Steinkamp* had an office at 80 W. Court Street, which he shared with his son, *Joseph G. Steinkamp*. However, Joseph soon found himself working on his own for the first time, following the death of his father in 1890.[5] Later, in 1896, Joseph moved his office to 24 E. Court Street[6], and the following year he took on his younger brother, Bernard, as a partner. The two formed *Joseph G. Steinkamp and Bro, Architects and Superintendents*.[7]

Architects who took on large projects, as the brothers did, often found it difficult to work alone or with a single partner.[8] Given that the brothers usually worked on several large and small projects at the same time, Joseph and Bernard partnered with architects *C. (Cecil) Howard Gillespie* (1896-1974) and *Nelson Felsberg* (1899–1979) for a number of years.[9] In addition, according to one report, Cincinnati architect *Henry E. Henthorn* also worked with the brothers at one time.[10]

Following the completion of the Mercantile Library Building that they designed, Joseph and Bernard Steinkamp occupied rooms 1211 to 1214 of the new building.[11] A notice in *The Western Architect and Builder* in 1904 stated that Joseph G. Steinkamp and Bro. were moving from their office on Court Street to the twelfth floor of the Mercantile Library building effective on April 30.[12] Although the firm had a suite of offices in the new building, little is known about the workings of the office. They must have had some draftsmen and probably some tracers to assist with their work, but there is no mention of the makeup of the office. Trade publications such as *The Ohio Architect and Builder* and *The American Contractor* typically referred to them as "preparing plans" for various types of structures. However, it is not clear whether all the planned structures were actually built.

Many of the newly completed Mercantile Library Building occupants, in addition to the Steinkamp brothers, were architects, builders, realtors, lawyers, and other professionals. Over the next several years, the brothers designed homes and places of business for many of the men who had their offices in the building. Did it go something like this on the morning ride up the elevator? "Mr. Steinkamp (could it have been "Joe" or "Bernie") I'm planning on building a new home in Walnut Hills. Would you be interested in designing it?" What often transpired is that the Steinkamps would design a home and a factory for businessmen. In some cases, the home came first, and in others, it was the factory.

In addition to designing homes for many local businessmen, the brothers also designed many practical homes for tradesmen. For example, it was not uncommon to see them designing a home for a stone mason and then to see that stone mason working on a home for another worker. Often these homes were one- or two-family homes of two and one-half stories. In fact, the brothers designed dozens of such buildings around the city.

While many of their buildings remain standing and can be confirmed, others have been lost to the wrecking ball. For example, they designed several buildings on Longworth Street in the downtown area, where the Duke Energy Convention Center is now situated, and those along Burnet Street have been replaced by hospital buildings. The firm remained in the Mercantile Library until around 1945, although they relocated within the building a few times, possibly downsizing over the years.[13,14]

Joseph and Bernard designed many types of structures, from small private homes to large, modern apartment buildings and even skyscrapers. Many of the large apartment buildings were in collaboration with the Emery family. *Thomas L. Emery* made a fortune in industries based on pork by-products when he found that the lard discarded from Cincinnati's prodigious meat industry could be converted into candles and lamp oil in the days before electric lights. He was also successful in real estate and manufacturing at the time of his accidental death in 1857. His sons—*John J. Emery, Sr.* (1834–1908), *Thomas J. Emery* (1830–1906), and *J. Howard Emery* (1838–1886)—continued and developed the family business under the name *Thomas Emery & Sons*, although the company was often referred to as *Thomas Emery's Sons*.[15] In the 1870s and 1880s, the Emerys worked with noted Cincinnati architect *Samuel Hannaford* in developing many fine buildings in the city. Johann (J. B.) Steinkamp worked as a superintendent on some of the Hannaford-designed buildings. It is known that they collaborated on the first building constructed on the University of Cincinnati campus, in 1875.[16] By most accounts, after the partial collapse of the Palace Hotel, which was designed by Hannaford, the Emerys took on the Steinkamps as their primary architects.

Thomas Emery's Sons had built Cincinnati's first apartment buildings, with suites of three to five rooms all on one floor, which they called "flats."[17] Joseph and Bernard collaborated with the Emery family on a number of large apartment buildings over a span of about 30 years.

The Steinkamps were also involved with Thomas Emery's widow, Mary, the founder of Mariemont, and designed a massive theater complex for Mariemont; however, the Steinkamps along with a number of architects were removed from the project, and the complex was never built.[18] Many of the large apartment buildings for the Emery family were downtown and in the inner suburbs, such as Avondale, Walnut Hills, and Clifton, usually on streetcar lines. They also designed quite a few four-story apartment buildings that had retail shops on the first floor and apartments on the upper three. Over the span of almost 50 years, they designed close to 300 buildings—from stables to garages and auto dealerships to private homes to movie theaters, banks, schools, churches, and high-rise office buildings—in the Cincinnati area and beyond.

Johan Herman Heinrich Steinkamp

1-1. Old St. Mary's Church in Downtown Cincinnati, ca. **1841** [21]

Johan Herman Heinrich Steinkamp was born in April 1786 in Nellinghof in the Duchy of Oldenberg, Germany, and married Maria Elizabet Kramer in 1822. They emigrated to North America in 1835 with four of their children.[19] Johan supervised the construction of Old St. Mary's Church in Over-The-Rhine in 1841, although Herbert stated that Bernard had been the superintendent.[20] As the story is told, the parishioners took home the bricks used to build the church to bake them in their ovens. One of Johan and Maria's children was Joannes Bernard Steinkamp, born in 1827.

Johann went by several names in the United States, including *J.B. Steinkamp, John B. Steinkamp, and Bernard Joseph Steinkamp*. However, he was often referred to as J. B. Steinkamp

1-2. Johann Steinkamp [22,a]

in U.S. trade publications. Johann was trained as a carpenter and then worked as superintendent of construction for the Emery family, among others, and practiced as an architect ca. 1880–1890. The earliest known work of Johann Steinkamp on record was for the first building constructed for the *University of Cincinnati* campus in 1875. He was paid $650 ($14,000 in today's dollars) "for superintendence of University building."[16] In 1880, he had an office at 174 Race Street, but in 1885 he moved to 80 W. Court Street and practiced architecture there until his death on February 7, 1890.[5] During the 1880s and early 1890s, J.B. and then Joseph, after his father's death, designed several flats for the Emery family. These were typically four stories with retail space on the first floor and apartments above, although one was seven stories. Unfortunately, information about these buildings is limited.

Johann married Mary Elizabeth Ahrens (1839–1926)[23] and they had 12 children:

Catharina (Kathrine, Catherine) (Poetker) (1862–1961)

Elizabeth Anna Maria (Oftholthoff) (1864–1943)

Anna (Annie) (1867–1943)

Joseph Gerhard (1868–1948)

Francis (Frank) Heinrich (1871–xxxx)

Bernard Johan (1876–1943)

Rosa (Rosie, Rose) (1879–xxxx) (Schneider)

George Joseph (1884–1961)

Luisa Maria (Mary)

Carolina Maria

Maria (Mary)

Cäcilia (Cecelia, Celia) Clara

In 1880, the family was living at 162 E. Liberty Street in the downtown area.[19, 24, 25]

---

[a] In the article about Johann and Joseph Steinkamp, the photo is titled Jos. G. Steinkamp. However, at the time of the publication, Joseph would have been a much younger man (33 years old) than the one depicted in the photo. One can only assume that it is a photo of Johann.

1-3. Steinkamp stained-glass window in Old St. Mary's Church [28]

Johann supervised the construction of the Grand Hotel, the old Queen City Club, and the old Emery Arcade.[9] Following in his father's work on Old St. Mary's Church, he was one of the parishioners involved with an 1890s renovation for its Golden Jubilee celebration. His name appears on one of the 12 large stained-glass windows on Old St. Mary's Church as "Bernard Steinkamp."[26] The date of his birth on the window is correct, but the date listed for his death is 1906, which is not correct. Johann's widow, Elizabeth, continued to live in the family home on E. Liberty Street. On Christmas Day, 1921, several members of the Steinkamp family gathered to celebrate Elizabeth's eighty-second birthday.[27] She passed away in April 1926 and her son, Reverend George Steinkamp, officiated at a Solemn Requiem Mass for her at St. Mary's Church.[23]

Joseph Gerhard Steinkamp

1-4. Joseph G. Steinkamp, ca. 1903 [31]

Joseph Gerhard Steinkamp, born October 15, 1868, received his elementary and college preparatory training in parochial schools before attending St. Xavier College (now Xavier University) and graduating from the Ohio Mechanics' Institute. He first worked in the office of his father, Johann, but after his father died, he worked on his own as the youngest architect in Cincinnati. When his younger brother, Bernard F. Steinkamp, joined him around 1897, the firm became known as Joseph G. Steinkamp & Brother.[5, 29, 30]

In June 1895, Joseph married Laura M. Menke (1874–1944), daughter of Elizabeth and former state senator John B. Menke, and they lived on McMillian Street.[5, 29, 30] Three months before their wedding in June of that year, Joseph gave his bride-to-be a beautiful gold pocket watch. It was inscribed "From Joe to Laura, March 18, 1895" and was made by the Waltham Watch

1-5, 1-6, 1-7. Joseph's gift to Laura

Company in Waltham, Massachusetts. The face of the watch was adorned with beautiful gold decorations and the cover was decorated with flowers surrounding a small church on a hill.[32]

Joseph and Laura had two sons, Albert (1896–1963) and Eugene (1903–1982).[5, 29, 30, 33, 34] In 1902, the family moved to **912 Suire Avenue** in Price Hill and Joseph designed an addition on the south side of the house.[5, 35] In 1927, he bought the two adjoining lots on the north side of this house from Marion L. Suire.[36] During the next year he designed his unique home, at **916 Suire Avenue**, that was completed in 1928. He tried to sell the house at 912 Suire and then almost immediately put his new house on the market.[37] Starting in May of 1928, he placed several ads in the *Cincinnati Enquirer,* trying to sell his new home.[37–41] Unfortunately for Joseph and his family, his lovely new home at 916 Suire Avenue was sold at auction in December 1929 for $16,3000, and the family resumed residence at 912 Suire.[42, 43]

In 1934, Joseph and Laura moved into a house on **Anderson Ferry Road** in Delhi Township.[44] Although there is no account of his doing so, he most likely designed their new home.[45] Following Bernard's passing in 1943 and Laura's sudden death in 1944, Joseph moved in with his son Albert, who lived on Relleum Avenue in Price Hill.[46–48] At that time, Joseph's other son, Eugene, lived a short distance away on Coronado Avenue.[49] In 1945, Joseph had an office in Proust Corner, 4900 Glenway Avenue, just around the corner from Albert's home.[50] Towards the end of the 1930s, Joseph and Bernard, along with Felsberg and Gillespie, designed several commercial buildings and homes. The only collaboration the brothers appear to have had after 1940 was the design of two apartment buildings for Bernard, presumably as investment properties.[51, 52]

Joseph spent the last year of his life in St. Joseph's Hospital and passed away at the age of 80 on October 21, 1948. His obituary was printed in several newspapers, including the *Cincinnati Enquirer, The New York Times,* the *Cincinnati Post, The Journal Herald,* and *The Newark Advocate.*[53–57] His brother, Father George Steinkamp, sang a requiem solemn mass at St. William Church that he and Bernard had designed in Price Hill. Joseph was buried in St. Mary's Cemetery in St. Bernard, Ohio.[58]

Little has been written about Joseph's life beyond his work as an architect. During his lifetime, he was described as a "progressive republican who looks beyond the old and conservative methods and seeks out new plans for political action in keeping with the spirit of advancement of the age." He was a member of St. William Church, a member of the Knights of Columbus, whose Price Hill meeting place his firm also designed, and a member of the Art Club and the Automobile Club.[59] When the Automobile Club sponsored an annual outing for Cincinnati orphans in 1912, Joseph and Bernard provided their own cars for the more than 1500 orphans on this festive day.[60]

In 1890, it was reported that Joseph was a member of the St. Stanislaus' Young Men's Association of St. Mary's Church and took part in a dramatic presentation called "A Race for Dinner" at the Odean Theater on the day after Christmas.[61] Joseph appropriately played *Measurton*, an architect.

Joseph appears to have had a difficult time getting used to driving early automobiles. In 1913 and again in 1915, it was reported in The *Cincinnati Post* that Joseph was involved in two mishaps.[62, 63] The first was when he ran over and seriously injured a 12-year-old boy on Seton Avenue. Reverend Father Roth of St. William Church was riding with Steinkamp and carried the unconscious boy to a neighbor's home where he was attended to by a doctor. In the second, Joseph's car was struck by another vehicle on Eighth Street in a multicar accident. Joseph was able to drive the injured driver of the other vehicle to the hospital for treatment of a broken leg.

In 1924, at a meeting of the Automobile Club, Joseph expressed his displeasure with the city ordinance concerning streetcar safety zones. As he stated in the *Cincinnati Enquirer*, "I notice the police have ruled that automobiles must keep out of the street car rails in the safety zone. Why should a vehicle be kept out of this zone when there is no street car in the zone?"[64] During World War I, Joseph served on all the loan drives and Red Cross drives and surrendered his offices to government officials. He was involved in railroad construction work until the end of the war.[65] However, there appears to be no record of the work for the railroad, and the brothers still managed to design a few buildings during wartime.

One rare mention of Joseph's personal life in the press was when he and some friends enjoyed a beach party in Ft. Lauderdale, Florida, in 1930, apparently without Mrs. Steinkamp.[66]

Unfortunately, in January 1941, Laura Steinkamp, then about 62 years old, fell while shopping in Kresge's Five and Ten Cent Store on Fifth Street in downtown Cincinnati. Mrs. Steinkamp was alleged to have fallen down 15 steps after slipping on the smooth stairs.[67] Who better to know that the stairs and railings did not meet the city's building code than the person who had been the Chair of the Cincinnati Building Code Commission and had advised the Mayor of Cincinnati on their adoption?[68, 69] Joseph brought a suit against the **S. S. *Kresge Company*** alleging that he had to do all the work about the house and was unable to work as an architect, causing his income to stop, and was unable to pay normal expenses and bills incurred by his wife's injuries. In the lawsuit, Joseph sought the sum of $5,000. In May of 1943, the Court of Common

Pleas in Hamilton County ruled in favor of the S.S. Kresge Company and Joseph was ordered to pay the court costs.[70] The extent of Laura's injuries is not known, and she passed away about a year later from a stroke.[71]

Joseph was a member of the St. Aloysius Orphan Society for over fifty years and was honored at the annual orphans' feast in 1943. Joseph's nephew, Lawrence A. Poetker, husband of Katherine and a Cincinnati attorney, was president of the St. Aloysius Orphanage.[72]

Professional Life

Joseph Steinkamp was an active member of the ***Cincinnati Chapter, American Institute of Architects*** (AIA), and was involved in developing building codes for the city of Cincinnati and state of Ohio. Joseph served the AIA in various capacities: as treasurer of the Cincinnati chapter in 1911, as secretary of the chapter in 1913 and 1914, and as president of the chapter from 1921 to 1924.[73-75] From time-to-time, he was called upon by the City to act as an expert witness in matters related to design and building codes. In 1908, the Cincinnati City Council appointed Joseph, A. T. Hazen, and Frank Dinsmore as a commission to draft a new building code for the city. They received $500 each for their work.[76] Joseph chaired the Commission in 1908 and 1909.[77]

Joseph was involved with the formation of the ***Ohio State Association of Architects*** in 1915 and was president of the association in 1920. The association was active in recommending to the General Assembly of the State of Ohio the enactment of a state building code.[78, 79]

In 1902, Joseph was one of several prominent architects from Cincinnati who were invited to Indianapolis, Indiana, by William F. Behrens to view his work on the interior of the Columbia Club and the new Claypool Hotel. The architects were given a tour of the city and the hotel and enjoyed a dinner on the roof of the Columbia Club so thoroughly that they decided to spend the night in Indianapolis.[80]

Following a fatal 1908 fire in the Neave Building at the corner of Fourth and Race Streets in Downtown Cincinnati, Joseph Steinkamp, as Chairman of the Building Code Commission, commented on the lack of fire escapes in the building and the provisions in the proposed building code that would address future fires and help prevent deaths and injuries.[81] The following year, Joseph, as the Building Code Commissioner, along with the City Solicitor explained the new building code to Mayor Galvin before he signed it into law.[82]

Joseph G. Steinkamp and Bro. were one of several architectural firms to exhibit at an architectural exhibition sponsored by the Cincinnati Chapter of the AIA that was held at the Cincinnati Art Museum in 1908.[83]

Joseph was one of several local architects who represented the local chapter of the AIA at the fiftieth annual convention in Washington, DC, in January of 1906.[84]

Interestingly, ten members of the local chapter of the AIA, including Joseph, practically

1-8. Joseph G. Steinkamp, ca. 1913 [88]

went on strike in 1914 when they claimed that competition rules were not being followed for the preparation of plans for a proposed high school in Hyde Park. They argued that the Board of Education would likely be compelled to select an architect without competition, resulting in the commission going to a non-resident architect.[85, 86]

Joseph took time out to write a 5-page article on building codes for *Building Management* in July 1913 which featured the photo of a distinguished-looking gentleman of about 45 years of age.[87]

An article in *Elementary Civics* in 1916 by Joseph was titled "Enforce Personal Responsibility."[88] The article noted a paper given by Steinkamp on "Building Codes" at the National Association of Building Managers 1913 convention.[89]

As chairman of the Legislative Committee of the Cincinnati Chapter of AIA, Joseph was a delegate to the AIA national convention in Washington, DC, in 1924.[90] In June of the same year, Joseph was appointed by the Superior Court as an expert "disinterested architect" to examine the plans for a proposed 11-story apartment building on Reading Road after a suit was brought to block its construction. Steinkamp reported that the building was designed by "one of the best structural engineers in the country," that the plans were sufficient in detail, and that the builders were bound to conform with the new building codes.[91] The following year, Joseph was again named as a delegate to a conference. This time, serving as a member of the United City Planning Committee, he attended the 1925 International Town, City, and Regional Planning Conference in New York City.[92]

Joseph took part in freshman orientation at St. Xavier College in April 1930, where he gave insight into the profession of architecture to the incoming class. The article noted that Joseph and his brother designed the layout of the campus, which had been praised "as being one of the most beautiful in the country." [93]

In January 1931, *The Xaverian News* published an article that highlighted a radio talk on WLW by Joseph G. Steinkamp during the Christmas holidays.[94] The article stated that the address merited so much praise and aroused so much comment that the *News* was induced to print part of the speech. In part, Steinkamp said:

> *As the principal functions of universities and colleges are to broaden the mind and to father and expound the truth, it is evident that the physical and visible properties, especially those relating to the architecture of their Halls, Libraries, Dormitories and the various units, should be sermons, poems and symphonies in aesthetics.*

Plans for beautifying the Laurel Street approach to the new Union Passenger Station were presented to the Cincinnati City Manager and the Director of Public Works by Joseph in January 1932. He proposed to beautify both sides of the approach either by remodeling existing one-family houses or constructing apartments of similar height.[95] The meeting was followed up by one in April explaining the beautification plans to more than 350 property owners in that section of the city. Joseph gave specific illustrations of what improvements could be made, and another meeting was planned to outline the definitive actions that would be put in place.[96]

In February of the same year, Joseph and several other noted Cincinnati architects were appointed by the mayor as members of a special committee to address concerns by attorneys for the Cincinnati Meat Packers Association and Cincinnati Wholesale Meat Packers Association, who vigorously objected to a new zoning ordinance and zoning territory.[97]

Joseph Steinkamp was among a delegation of architects from the Cincinnati Chapter of the AIA who inspected the almost completed Cincinnati Union Terminal in January 1933, just two months before its dedication. The terminal has been called the last great railroad station built in the United States and an Art Deco masterpiece.[98]

Possibly sensing the need for inexpensive housing during the Depression, it appears that in 1935 Joseph and Bernard promoted the design of a small home that could be purchased with little money down and modest monthly payments. They were joined in this effort by their associates Gillespie and Felsberg.[99]

1-9. Advertisement for small Early American Home [99]

In 1940, Joseph Steinkamp and two other prominent Cincinnati architects, *Gustave Drach* and *Harry Hake*, were honored for their many years of service at a dinner by the Cincinnati chapter of the AIA.[100]

Three veteran Cincinnati architects—left to right, Gustave Drach, Harry Hake, and Joseph Steinkamp—pore over an old photograph on display at the dinner given in their honor last night at the Hotel Gibson by Cincinnati Chapter, American Institute of Architects. Drach began practice in 1884, Hake in 1889, Steinkamp in 1890. On behalf of the chapter, Russell S. Potter presented certificates of their long service to the three.

1-10. American Institute of Architects Awards Night [100]

As a member and officer of the Cincinnati AIA chapter throughout his career, Joseph was made member emeritus of the AIA, as reported by chapter president George F. Roth in 1941.[101] The *Cincinnati Enquirer* quoted Mr. Roth on July 4th, 1941, as stating "Aside from Mr. Steinkamp's professional works, which include a number of outstanding buildings in the vicinity, he has been very active in the development and study of building codes and ordinances, having assisted the Cincinnati government in the formation of these regulations." Mr. Roth concluded, "The member emeritus rating is bestowed upon only those persons whose past activity over many years has been of extreme value to the profession and who have reached the age of 70 years."

Bernard F. Steinkamp

Joseph's younger brother, Bernard, was born May 3, 1876. Like Joseph, he attended parochial schools and St. Xavier College. In 1900 he married Clara Sunderman (1879–1969), and they also had two sons, George A. (1901–1987) and Paul J. (1911–1984).[102] For a short time after their marriage, Bernard and Clara lived on Woodward Street[104] and then moved to *Clarion Avenue* in Evanston around 1908[105], where he lived until his death. Although there is no record of it, the brothers probably designed Bernard's

1-11. Bernard F. Steinkamp ca. 1903 [31]   **1-12.** Bernard F. Steinkamp ca. 1909 [103]

home. Bernard continued to work with Joseph until 1941 and passed away in 1943 at age 67.[106] He too was buried in St. Mary's Cemetery, following a requiem high mass at St. Mark's Church in Evanston that he helped design.[107] Clara outlived her husband by a number of years, passing away in May 1969.[108]

Even less is known about Bernard's life outside his work with Joseph. When Bernard was mentioned in the newspaper, it was a mix of good and bad news. In 1907, the *Cincinnati Enquirer* reported that a "Mr. Steinkamp" who was associated with the Bismark [sic] Café (Joseph and Bernard had designed the Bismarck Café in the Mercantile Library Building[109]) had secured the Wefler Grounds baseball park and he was planning to tear down the old stands and build new ones behind home plate for the new Oakley Park. Mr. Steinkamp was described as a lover of baseball and guaranteed the best of treatment for visiting teams.[112] A few years later, reports in the *Enquirer* mentioned amateur baseball games at the "Oakley-Steinkamp's Park" or "Steinkamp's Park" in Oakley.[110] Although the identity of Mr. Steinkamp was not made clear in the article, it may have been Bernard, since his son Paul was an outstanding athlete at St. Xavier College.

Unfortunately, it was later reported that in 1912, while working on the Castellini home in Hyde Park, Bernard fell and broke his arm.[113] He was even incorrectly referred to as "Benjamin" Steinkamp, a mistake that seemed to follow him during his lifetime. On a lighter note, Bernard took part in "Stunt Night," described as a "Merry Annual Frolic," as a member of the Cincinnati Club in a "Bathing Beauty Contest" in April 1930.[114]

In May 1935, it was announced that Bernard E. *[sic]* Steinkamp would be attending a school of the Federal Housing Administration in preparation for his appointment to the District Director's office.[115] In an article that he wrote about insurance rates for the *Cincinnati Enquirer*, Bernard was identified as Chief Architecture Supervisor of the Federal Housing Administration, Southern Ohio District.[117] On February 7, 1936, it was reported that he was mistakenly identified as the supervising architect of the National Home Show at the Music Hall in Cincinnati on the previous day.[117, 118]

Bernard's family gave rise to several future architects. ***Mark Steinkamp***, a great grandson of Bernard, is Vice President and Owner at Kennington Design Build Inc. in Albuquerque, New Mexico.[119] ***Robert G. Steinkamp***, Bernard's grandson, was a partner in Steinkamp and Nordloh in Milford, Ohio, and later a partner in Steinkamp, Steinkamp and Hampton, also in Milford, with his son ***Robert J. Steinkamp***.[120, 121]

The Steinkamps' collaborators, ***Nelson Felsberg*** and ***C. Howard Gillespie***, continued working as architects for a number of years. Both were involved with designing several buildings for the Hudepohl Brewing Company and other buildings in the Cincinnati area. Felsberg continued working until his death in 1979 and made a generous bequest of $30,000 to the AIA, which helped establish the *Architectural Foundation of Cincinnati* in 1982.[122] Not very much is known about Gillespie. He and his son purchased radio station KXGI in Ft. Madison, Iowa, in 1939, and, after they parted ways with the Steinkamps, he collaborated with Felsberg from 1939 to 1958.[123]

Reverend George J. Steinkamp

Joseph's and Bernard's younger brother, ***Reverend George J. Steinkamp***, was a prominent Catholic priest and deserves mention as he had some influence on their work. He was born March 19, 1884. As a young boy he studied at St. Mary's parochial school in Cincinnati, and he graduated from St. Xavier College in 1904.[124] He studied for the priesthood at St. Mary's Seminary in Dayton and was ordained in 1908, after which he was an assistant pastor at St. Mary's Church. Father Steinkamp was appointed pastor of St. Paul's parish in Yellow Springs, Ohio, in 1917[125], and two years later he transferred to St. John Church in Edgemont, Ohio, where he served for nine years. In 1928, he became pastor of Our Lady of Mercy Church in North Riverdale.[126]

While Father Steinkamp was assistant pastor of St. Mary's Church, Joseph and Bernard designed a school for the congregation that originally cost $40,000 but grew to $50,000.[127, 128] When he served as pastor of St. John Church, his brothers designed the new St. John School, in 1923.[129, 130] A few years later, in 1930, when their brother was at Our Lady of Mercy Church, they designed a new church for that parish as well.[131]

Father Steinkamp often travelled from Dayton to Cincinnati to officiate at family weddings, such as his nephew George's wedding to Martha Berning in 1926 and his nephew Paul's wedding to Amanda Tassinger in 1936.[133, 134] He also officiated at funerals for several family members, including Joseph.

1-13. Reverend George J. Steinkamp, ca. 1917 [125]

1-14. Reverend George J. Steinkamp, ca. 1961 [132]

Two of his sisters, *Anna* and *Cecelia*, never married and kept house for Father Steinkamp in Dayton until Anna's passing in 1943.[135, 136] George outlived both Joseph and Bernard, passing away in December of 1961.[137]

Other Steinkamp Siblings

Not much information is available about some of the remaining Steinkamp siblings. As mentioned earlier, sisters *Anna* and *Cecelia* never married and kept house for *Father George Steinkamp* during most of their brother's tenure in Dayton.

Elizabeth married Henry Ostholhoff and they lived at 546 E. Liberty Street. They had three children, the future Mrs. Raymond Rack, Henry G., and Bernard F. Ostholthoff. She passed away in December of 1943.[138]

Katherine (Catherine) married Henry Poetker and they had two sons: Lawrence A. Poetker a Cincinnati attorney who was president of the St. Aloysius Orphanage and the Reverend Albert H. Poetker, a physics and mathematics professor at Xavier University. Katherine and her husband lived near her sister Elizabeth at 524 E. Liberty Street. Katherine passed away in April of 1951.[139]

Rose married Frank J. Schneider. They lived at 530 E. Thirteenth Street.[140]

CHAPTER 2

Downtown Cincinnati

Although Joseph and Bernard Steinkamp were not responsible for some of the more glamorous buildings in downtown Cincinnati (as was Samuel Hannaford, who designed Music Hall, City Hall, and so many other fine buildings), the brothers designed the *Mercantile Library Building*, the *American Building*, and the *Metropole Hotel*. They also designed many other types of structures, from cold storage for the Castellini family, to garages, to high-end apartment buildings. In all, Johann, Joseph, and later Joseph and Bernard contributed to 50-some structures in the downtown area alone. Some are still standing and have been updated and repurposed, while others have met the fate of many historic buildings and have been demolished to make way for new construction.

Johann B. Steinkamp started working with the Emery family in the 1880s, designing apartment buildings in the downtown area of Cincinnati. Young Joseph had been a student at the Ohio Mechanics Institute around this time, but he soon joined his father in working with the Emerys and other clients. Following his father's death in 1890, Joseph took over on his own as the youngest architect in Cincinnati.[1] After a slowdown in construction during the First World War, business picked up, especially with the construction of automobile showrooms and garages. Fortunately, several of these have survived in the downtown area and have been repurposed into office buildings or restaurants.

Around the turn of the 20th century, there was a rather unusual street in downtown Cincinnati. It was between Fifth and Sixth Streets and was only a few blocks long, but it had four names. From Vine Street to Elm Street, it was known as Opera Place; from Elm to Plum Street, it was called Post Square; and from Plum to Central Avenue, it was known as Longworth Street. Finally, from Central to Baymiller Street, it was called Carlisle Avenue.[2] The Steinkamp brothers designed several buildings on Longworth Street, including some for J.J. Castellini, and others on Opera Place. Unfortunately, none of them survived, as the Duke Energy Convention Center now sits at this location.

The first mention of Joseph Steinkamp working in the downtown area was recorded in February 1882 when, following collapse of two walls during construction of *The Palace Hotel*, which was originally called the *Bradford Hotel*, Joseph Steinkamp was reported to have taken over construction. At the time it was built, the eight-story structure was the tallest in Cincinnati. It was built in the French Second Empire style by *Thomas Emery and Sons* with *Samuel Hannaford* as the original architect.[3] The hotel was renamed *The Cincinnatian* in 1951. The partnership with the Emerys in 1882 appears to be the first project of many on which Joseph, and later Joseph and Bernard, collaborated with them. It was reported that the collapse at The Palace Hotel was due to the addition of a door that was not in the original plans.[4] However, a few days later, a scathing article appeared in the *Cincinnati Enquirer* condemning the Emerys for their shoddy workmanship, inferior materials, and willingness to cut corners to make as much of a profit as possible with little regard to safety.[5] Some prominent Cincinnati architects criticized the Emerys, and the Bradford family said they did not want the hotel named after them. Nevertheless, the hotel and many other structures built by the Emerys are still in use 130 years after they were built. In 1980, the Cincinnatian was added to the National Register of Historic Places.[6] More than 100 years and $25 million later, the building was reborn, opening in 1987 as the city's only small boutique hotel. The number of rooms dropped to 146 luxurious, spacious suites, and the soaring, eight-story atrium topped with a vast skylight serves as the Cincinnatian's focal point.[7]

2-1. The Palace Hotel, ca. 1882 [8]

2-2. The Cincinnatian Hotel [9]

2-3. The Savoy, 225 W. Court Street, ca. 1885

In 1885, Joseph, probably along with his father, designed an apartment in downtown Cincinnati for *Thomas Emery's Sons*. The *Savoy* on *W. Court Street* is a four-story apartment that is still in use today.[10]

They are also credited with designing the *Normandy Apartments* on the corner of *Race and Longworth Streets* in 1885.[10] However, an advertisement in the *Cincinnati Enquirer* in 1882 listed *Thomas Emery's Sons* as owners of the Normandy Flats at Race and Longworth Streets.[11] Ten years later, in 1892, it was reported in the *Enquirer* that the Emerys had recently purchased the Normandy Building and that Joseph was preparing plans for additions to the building.[12] It appears that the Emerys owned this building and that the Steinkamps worked on it, but the timeline is confusing. The Normandy Apartments were demolished along with the rest of Longworth Street.

2-4. Woodward Flats, 64 Woodward Street, ca. 1887

The year 1887 was a busy one for Johann and Joseph. Collaborating with *Thomas Emery's Sons*, the firm designed four buildings in the downtown area.[13] One was a *four-story flat at 340 W. Fifth Street* for $18,000 which was demolished to make way for the Duke Energy Convention Center. Another was a two and one-half-story home for *Herman Tapke* at a cost of $9,000. Mr. Tapke managed 184 Main Street in 1890, which is now the site of The Banks.[14] Two other buildings included a four-story flat for *G. Kuhlman* at 64 Woodward Street, which is currently the *Woodward Flats*, and another four-story store and flat on *Court Street*. This design was a common one the brothers employed in many other projects, with one or two stores on the first floor and apartments or flats on the upper three floors.

The following year, J.B. designed alterations and additions to the Emery residence in order to convert it into a flat building at a cost of $5,000.[15] This may have been the former home of *J.J. Emery at 301 W. Fourth*.[16]

In 1889, it was reported that J. B. Steinkamp designed a four-story tenement on **Pendleton Street** for *F. Kinker* that cost $7,000.[17] According to the *Williams' Cincinnati Directory*, Frank Kinker lived on E. Liberty, near Pendleton.[18] It appears to have been one of these two buildings.

2-5. Pendleton Street Apartments, ca. 1889

Also, in 1889, Johann designed an apartment for the *Emery Brothers* at the corner of *Forth and South Streets* at a cost of $40,000.[19] It must have been a substantial apartment. The cost today would be $1.1 million. However, in 1889, the only South Street in Cincinnati was in an industrial area near Gest Street, which would not be a suitable location for such an expensive apartment and its location is unknown. Since Johann passed away soon afterwards, this may have been one of the last projects he ever worked on.

The *Waldo Apartments* on the corner of Elm and Eighth Streets in downtown Cincinnati have also been known as the *Norfolk Apartments* and the *Talbot Apartments*.[4] Built ca. 1890[20], the building reportedly was named after Ralph Waldo Emerson. Like some buildings of this era, it has been attributed to Joseph Steinkamp[4] but also to Samuel Hannaford.[21]

2-6. The Waldo Apartments, Eighth and Elm Streets, ca. 1890 [22]

2-7. The Waldo Apartments, ca. 2008 [23]

2-8. San Rafael Apartments, Fourth Street, ca. 1890 [28]

The *San Rafael Apartments*, built ca. 1890 on *Fourth Street* in downtown Cincinnati[24], have been attributed to Joseph Steinkamp.[4, 25] Additionally, the *Cincinnati Enquirer* reported that the five-story addition to the apartments was commissioned by *Thomas Emery's Sons* in 1894, with Joseph as the architect.[26] In 1930 the apartment was listed in the *Cincinnati Enquirer* as "Colored Only" and in 1935, the building was sold at auction.[27] The San Rafael was eventually demolished after 1950.

The *Cincinnati Enquirer* reported two years later that Joseph was designing *a four-story store and flats building* on *Central Avenue* near Court Street. The article did not mention the name of the owner, but it gave the cost of the apartment at $15,000.[29] It appears to be one of these four buildings, possibly the one on the right in the photo.

2-9. Central Avenue apartment, ca. 1892 [30]

Joseph took on the task of designing a flat building for the *Hon. Edward A. Ferguson* at the corner of *Dayton Street and Freeman Avenue* in 1892.[31] Mr. Ferguson, a lawyer and state senator, was called "The Father of the Cincinnati Southern Railroad" as the author of the Cincinnati Southern Railway Act that made it possible for the city to own a railroad.[32] The building was eventually demolished around 1912 to make room for an updated flat.[33]

Joseph Steinkamp is listed as the architect for another four-story store and flats at *312 W. Fifth Street* in downtown. It was built in 1893 for *G. H. Verkamp*, the oldest clothing manufacturing establishment in Cincinnati, for $6,000.[34, 35] An ad in the *Xaverian News* shows that G. H. Verkamp & Sons sold men's and boys' clothing at their store.[36] The Duke Energy Convention Center is now at this site. Henry Poetker, the husband of the brothers' sister, Catherine, was employed by G. H. Verkamp for many years.

2-10. G. H. Verkamp Clothing Store, ca. 1893 [37]

Also, in 1893, Joseph designed another store and flat, this time for *J. H. Lippelman* at a cost of $8,000.[38] The location of the flat building was not given, but H. H. Lippelman of Glendale, who was a member of the Board of Control, had a business at *418 Sycamore Street* in 1900.[39] H. H. Lippleman was in the distilling business in addition to being a former County Commissioner.[40]

Still on his own in 1895, Joseph drew up plans for a four-story flat building for the *Orr estate* located at *24 W. Court Street*. It contained two stores and 12 three-room flats.[41, 42] It has recently been restored and serves as a restaurant and office space.

2-11. Orr Building, 24 W. Court Street, ca. 1895 [42]

2-12. Orr Building, ca. 2020

When Bernard joined the firm in 1897, the brothers designed another four-story building with retail on the first floor and flats on the upper floors. This building was at *Sixth and John Streets*, which, although they once intersected, they no longer do. It was owned by the *Perrin Estate* and was built at a cost of $10,000.[43]

The *Courtland Flats* (*Sandheger Flats*) were built on Court Street for *Christopher Sandheger* in the Second Renaissance Revival style in 1902. Joseph and Bernard were responsible for the design.[44] Sandheger had at one time partnered with Louis Hudepohl of the famous Cincinnati brewing family. Around the turn of the century, Cincinnati was the country's leader in whiskey production and Sandheger was one of Cincinnati's leading distillers of whiskey, which made him a very wealthy man.[45] The building was listed on the National Register of Historic Places in 1984.[46]

2-13. Courtland Flats, 117–121 E. Court Street, ca. 1902 [47]

2-14. Courtland Flats, ca. 2020

The brothers' early 20th-century works include the *Young Men's Mercantile Library Building*, which was built in 1902–1903 for the *Emery Estate*. A 1902 article in the *Cincinnati Enquirer* talks about the plans for the 12-story building, noting that "… it will be entirely surrounded by open spaces that will provide light at all times." The article concluded by stating that "…the square of Walnut Street, on the completion of the Traction Building and the Mercantile Library Building, will be the finest in the city."[48] It has been reported that a rendering of the building was delineated by John Scudder Adkins, a fine Beaux-Arts architect of Weber, Werner, and Adkins who may actually have been responsible for the design.[4] In 1903, it was reported that the plans for the library building had been filed with the Building Inspector and it was estimated that the building would cost at least $500,000. The building was to contain "…a large saloon and café and six stores on the first floor."[49]

Starting in 1904, the Steinkamps originally occupied a suite of offices on the twelfth floor for a number of years and moved to other locations in the building until around 1945, when Joseph vacated the building following Bernard's death. Interestingly, several architectural books from Joseph Steinkamp's collection are still on library reading room shelves. Having been granted a 10,000-year lease for the library, it currently occupies the eleventh and twelfth floors of the building. It is one of nearly two-dozen surviving membership libraries in the United States.[50] In February 2021, the Mercantile Library Building was granted a Local Historic Landmark Designation.[51]

2-15. Sketch of the proposed Mercantile Library Building [48]

2-16. Mercantile Library Building, 414 Walnut Street, ca. 1903 [52]

In 1904, the brothers gave the contract for the *Bismarck Café* in the Mercantile Library Building to *W.F. Beherns & Company*, decorators.[53] After a shaky start, the Bismarck became "…one of the largest establishments of its kind in Cincinnati and served the higher class trade." The establishment was divided into three large departments: The Lady's Grill, Grill Room, and Gentlemen's Room/Rathskeller.[54]

2-17. Dining Room in the Bismarck Café in the Mercantile Library Building [54]

In 1904, the brothers designed an *office and store on Eighth Street* for a *Mr. Boyle*.[55] This was most likely A.S. Boyle of 1908 W. Eighth Street[56], for whom the Steinkamps designed a new facility in Evanston in 1913.[57]

It has been reported that the *Sterling Glass Company* built their factory on the site of the former Highland House in Mt. Adams in 1902. Shortly afterwards, *The Western Architect & Builder* reported in 1904 that Joseph G. Steinkamp and Bro. were designing a 20,000 square foot factory for the company to be built after the foundation ruins of the Highland House were removed. The building was reported to be two stories with a large room where the company's products could be displayed and to cost "thousands of dollars."[58]

2-18. The Sterling Cut Glass Company, Mt. Adams, ca. 1902 [59]

Although the *Cincinnati Post* reported that the brothers designed a two and one-half story building on *Pendleton Street* near *Dandridge* for *Louis Massmann* in 1904, no Louis Massmann is listed on Pendleton.[60] It was also cited as being for A. Massmann and to cost $4,000.[61] A. Massman was listed at 1320 Pendleton, on the corner of Dandridge, which is two and one-half stories.[62]

2-19. 1320 Pendleton Street, ca. 1904 [63]

The brothers designed one of at least three stores for *B. H. Kroger* in 1904 in downtown Cincinnati. They also designed one on Reading Road and one in Kentucky. The exact location of the downtown store is difficult to locate as it was reported to be at *430 Main Street*[64] and *420 Main Street*[65], but the *Williams' Cincinnati Directory* has it at *530 Main Street* in 1910.[66] Additionally, an article in the *Cincinnati Enquirer* in 1908 has it on *Fifth Street* between Main and Sycamore Streets.[67] Either there were two Kroger stores close to each other or the locations were incorrect.

Also, working for the *Kroger Grocery and Baking Company* in 1904, they designed a seven-story building at *522 Hunt Street* (now Reading Road) that was to be used exclusively for baking and was to cost $25,000, a substantial amount in 1904.[68] At the time, Hunt Street ran from Main to Broadway.

The former home of Francis Hurtt, at the corner of *Dayton and Baymiller Streets* in Cincinnati's West End, was purchased by *Max Duechscher* around 1904. Joseph Steinkamp and Brother were the architects for the remodeling of the main building and designing the addition along Baymiller Street.[69] The two buildings combined had 18 flats with a total of 63 rooms and this is the only home on the street with a Mansard roof. This area of Dayton Street was known as "Millionaires' Row" for the prominent industrialists who resided in a row of opulent mansions built between 1850 and 1890.[70]

2-20. Addition to 850 Dayton Street, ca. 1904

2-21. Front of 850 Dayton Street, ca. 1904

That same year, Joseph and Bernard designed a three-story brick house on *E. Clifton Avenue* for *Mr. Daniel Cherdron* at a cost of $5,000.[71]

The brothers prepared plans for a seven-story brick building at the corner of *Longworth and Race Streets* in 1905. It was being built for *Greg G. Wright & Son* and was to cost $30,000.[72] However, it may have consisted of only four stories initally, because the brothers designed three stories to be added to the building in 1909.[73]

2-22. 220 E. Clifton, ca. 1904

2-23. Greg G. Wright & Son, ca. 1905 [74]

Also that year, Joseph and Bernard designed the *Cracker Bakery* for *Kroger Grocery & Baking Co*, located at *521 Reading Road*, where a casino now resides. The cost of the bakery was $40,000.[75, 76] The chain had grown to 40 stores by 1902, when it was incorporated as Kroger Grocery and Baking Co. This store, the one downtown, and the one they designed in Newport, Kentucky[77] were part of the rapid expansion in the Cincinnati area and beyond, which grew to almost 6,000 stores by 1929.[78]

2-24. Typical Kroger Grocery and Baking Co. Store, ca. 1910 [79]

The brothers were reported to have designed a two-story building to house the *William Seivers [sic] Mineral Water Works* in 1905 [80], which was located on *Spring Grove Avenue*[a]. Mr. Sievers lived at 1724 Hunt Street, now Reading Road.[81]

In 1906, the brothers designed a three and one-half story flat and store building at *324 E. Fourth Street* for *Telford and Groesbeck*, owners of the Johnson Building which was to cost $7,500.[82] Currently there is a three-story building at 324 E. Fourth Street which was reported to have been built in 1865.[83]

In what was probably their first time working with the *Hudepohl Brewing Company*, the Steinkamps designed a remodel and a new addition to the existing building at the corner of *Fifth and Pike Streets* in 1906 to cost $3,000.[84]

The brothers designed a building for *George R. Harris*, a real estate agent who had his office in the Mercantile Library Building, in 1907. It was a four-story apartment on *Findlay Street*.[85]

2-25. 128 Findlay Street, ca. 1907

[a] The notice in *Engineering News*, in addition to misspelling Mr. Sievers' name, lists the address for the William Seivers Mineral Water Works as being on Reading Road. However, his home was on Reading Road and the business was on Spring Grove Avenue.

In 1907 the *William Windhorst Company* dry good store at *Twelfth and Main Streets* was partially destroyed by a fire that claimed one life.[86] The following year, it was reported that Joseph and Bernard were completing plans for a five-story building to replace the one damaged in the fire, reportedly at a cost of between $25,000 and $50,000.[87, 88] However, the original and replacement structures contained only four stories.

2-26. William Windhorst Company, 1201 Main Street, ca. 1907

Still in 1907, Joseph and Bernard designed a two-story addition to the *Cordesman-Rechtin Company* at *215 Butler Street* at a cost of $3,000.[89] The building was located across from the Pittsburgh, Cincinnati, Chicago, and St. Louis Railroad Company Depot.[90] The following year the Steinkamps designed a home for Louis E. Rechtin, President and General Manager of the company, in Walnut Hills.[91]

2-27. Advertisement for Cordesman-Rechtin Company [92]

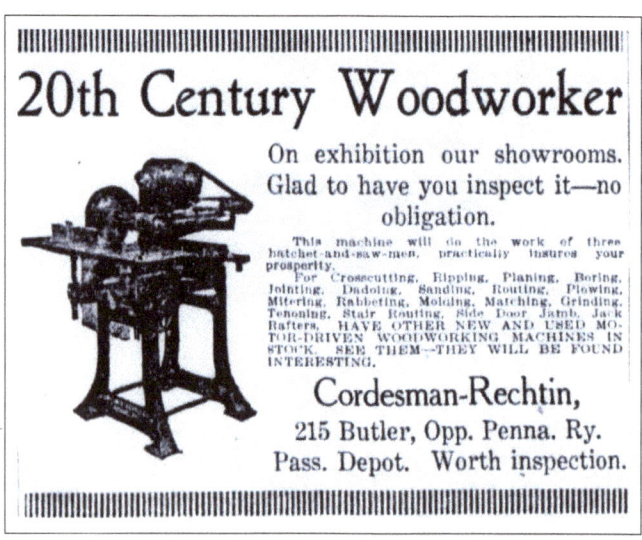

The Steinkamp brothers had both a business and personal relationship with the Siefke family. In 1907, they designed a new funeral parlor on the corner of *Eighth and Linn Streets* for *F. & W. Siefke*.[93, 94] It was a four-story building with apartments on the upper three floors and cost about $35,000. A few years later, they would design a home for Ed Siefke in Delhi and then one for W.G. Siefke in Hyde Park. Ed Siefke was married to Joseph's sister-in-law, Martha Menke Siefke.

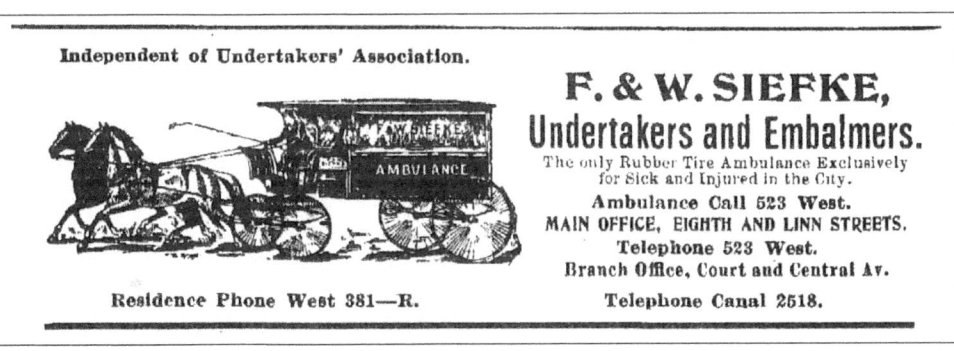

2-28. Advertisement for F. & W. Siefke [95]

The same year, the Steinkamps were designing what must have been substantial cattle sheds for the *Union Stock Yards Company* at the corner of *Spring Grove Avenue and Hopple Street*, for a cost of $28,000–$30,000, that would cover two acres.[96, 97]

Starting in 1906, there appears to have been a flurry of building activity in an area of Opera Place. In 1906, the *Cincinnati Enquirer* reported that the *McDonald Printing Company* was building a six-story addition on the south side of *Opera Place* for $20,000 and Crapaey and Lamm were the architects.[98] However, the following year, the McDonald Printing Company was reported to be building a six-story building on the south side of Opera Place with the Steinkamps as the architects.[99]

The brothers were once again involved in designing a new building to replace one that had been destroyed by fire. This one was a two-story concrete building for the *Cincinnati Oil Works* at *529 Eggleston Avenue*.[100] However, the company was listed at 521 and 523 Eggleston in 1908.[101]

In 1908, the brothers designed a two-story factory warehouse for the *Pfau Manufacturing Company* at *Spring and Twelfth Streets* at a cost of $1,500.[102] The company's headquarters was located on Reading Road at this time.

Also in 1908, it was reported the brothers were designing a three-story building on *Eighth Street near Baymiller Street* for *Mr. Birkmeyer (or Birkemeyer)*. The first floor was to be a warehouse and the upper two floors, four-room apartments; it was to cost $10,000.[103] The following month it was reported they were designing a one-story post office station on *W. Eighth Street* for *Postmaster Frank Birkmeyer* that cost $3,000.[104, 105]

Again the same year, they designed a four-story brick tenement on *Bremen Street* between Twelfth and Thirteenth Streets for the builders *Neil and Wegelin* at a cost of $7,500.[106] Bremen Street was renamed Republic Street during World War I.[107]

In 1908, the brothers designed a four-story store and apartment building for *Frank Kirchner*, President and General Manager of the Kirchner Construction Company, which was located at *221 W. Ninth Street*.[108] Fortunately, this beautiful structure is still standing.

In 1909, the *Enquirer* reported that the *Murdock Printing Company* had just completed a seven-story building designed by the Steinkamps on the south side of *Opera Place* and next to the Greg G. Wright building that the Steinkamps also designed.[109]

Still in Opera Place in 1912, the Steinkamps drew new plans for a seven-story addition to *McDonald Printing Company* on the south side of *Opera Place*. It was to replace the uncompleted structure started by William P. Devon that was only planned for a four-story building and was not of sufficient strength for a seven-story building.[110] Two days later, it was reported that the McDonald Printing Company was constructing a seven-story manufacturing building at 105–107 Opera Place for $25,000.[111] In 1915, the address of the printing company was given as 107–117 Opera Place.[112]

2-29. 221 W. Ninth Street, ca. 1908

Since Opera Place was only one block long, some of these notices may have referred to the same building. The McDonald Company was a major printer in Cincinnati, and the Murdock Building was at 120 Opera Place, but the L.S. Murdock Printing Company was in one room on Main Street.[113] The sons of Andrew J. McDonald, founder of the printing company, donated the Andrew J. and Mary McDonald Memorial Library on the Xavier University campus in honor of their parents.[114]

In 1909, Joseph and Bernard designed the eight-story *Robertson Building* at the corner of *Race and W. Seventh Streets* for *Musco M. Robertson*, President of the Robertson Realty Company, that was first estimated to cost $50,000 but then increased to $100,000.[115–117] This is the same company for whom they designed the Robertson Apartments (later the Elberon Apartments) in Price Hill.[118] In repayment for a loan, Mr. Robertson gave William S. P. Oskamp free rent for one year for the Oskamp Jewelry Store. In 1916, the brothers converted the sixth floor of the Robertson Building into doctors' offices at a cost of $8,000.[119] The Robertson building is currently undergoing major renovations as a TownePlace Suites by Marriot.* This will breathe life into another historic downtown buildings.

2-30. The Robertson Building, Race and Seventh Streets, ca. 1909 [120]

Around 1909, Joseph and Bernard designed a building for the Catholic fraternal organization *Order of Alhambra* at *Walnut and Court Streets*.[121] The Alhambra Building was listed as being at 925 Walnut Street in 1902[122] and the work in 1909 appears to be a renovation to an existing building.[123]

In 1909, the Steinkamps designed a four-story addition to the aforementioned three-story ***Greg G. Wright & Son Company*** building, which they had designed in 1905.[124] The original Wright building was supposed to have been seven stories, but it's possible only four stories were built in 1905.[125]

In August of that year, the headline in the *Cincinnati Post* read, "Month of August Will Be Big One in Real Estate Business."[126] ***Mrs. Mary Emery*** declared the building at ***1520 Central Avenue*** to be an eyesore that must be torn down. Mrs. Emery announced that all the Emery tenements that were not modern in construction would be rebuilt within a short time. The new building was to be four stories and "…one of the most modern design, to conform with the new building code." However, despite its modernity, it did not have bathtubs.[127] Unfortunately, the new building fell into disrepair and was eventually demolished. There was also a report the same year that the building may have been at 1525 Central Avenue.[128]

Also, in the same article, ***Richard Crane***, a noted Cincinnati businessman involved in Catholic welfare work who was made a Knight Commander by Pope Pius XI[129], stated that he was going to tear down the tenement he owned on Mulberry Street and replace it with a modern building to enhance the value of the surrounding property. Mr. Crane enlisted the Steinkamps to design a three-story brick tenement house on ***Mulberry Street***. It was located between Sycamore and Main Streets and cost $5,500.[127, 130]

Later in 1924, Joseph attended a testimonial dinner celebrating Sir Richard's knighthood.[131] Most of the homes on this section of Mulberry Street are being replaced with new construction and Sir Richard's may have been one of them.

Completing their work in 1909, the Steinkamps designed with two more four-story apartment buildings for *Thomas Emery's Sons,* one at *312–314 E. Fifth Street* at a cost of $15,000[132] and another at *1525 Central Avenue* where the new football stadium now resides.[133]

In 1910, the brothers were again working for the *Emery Estate* on plans to convert the *Carter Hotel Building* at the corner of *Sixth and Race Streets* into office suites.[134] Apparently, the hotel had at one time been named the Queen City Hotel that was owned by Thomas Emery, but had closed the previous year.[135]

Towards the end of 1910, they designed a fireproof three-story factory for *Thomas E. Kennedy & Company*, manufacturers of printing presses, at *337 Main Street.*[136]

Construction began on the *Hotel Metropole* in 1912 in Cincinnati's business district on *Walnut Street. Joseph C. Thoms*, an attorney, was instrumental in the development of the new hotel, and the firm of Joseph G. Steinkamp and Brother was chosen to design it. The hotel contained a grand dining room, a rathskeller in the basement, and a Turkish bath that was advertised as the "finest Turkish Bath in the state." Metropole was a popular name for hotels in the 19th century. Hotel entrepreneurs in the United States used it in the early 1900s to create an aura of sophistication. In Ohio, Metropoles were also located in Dayton, Wellsville, and Columbus, in addition to Cincinnati.[137]

2-31. Sign advertising the Hotel Metropole

2-32. Hotel Metropole original, 609 Walnut Street, ca. 1912 [138]

"What Steinkamp achieved was magnificent, as the building had such outstanding features like a two-story curving staircase, an ornate grand ballroom, and a sprawling lobby defined by its gorgeous 12-foot ceilings."[139] Christened as the "Hotel Metropole," Thoms' fellow Cincinnatians were awestruck by his luxurious, ten-story establishment when it debuted on New Year's Eve in 1912. The excitement over the Hotel Metropole was so great that close to 800 people arranged to attend its grand opening."[139] A city directory began advertising the Metropole as "A home for the man away from home," with room rates from $1.00 to $2.50.

A large addition was added to the north side of the hotel, doubling its size, in 1924. The addition was designed by H.L. Stevens & Co., an architectural and engineering firm in Chicago. At this time, a mezzanine and a penthouse apartment were added, but the Turkish bath was demolished during the addition's construction.[137]

In 2009, the Hotel Metropole was added to the National Register of Historic Places[140], and it was reported that it would be converted to the *21c Museum Hotel*. In 2012, the award-winning 156-room boutique hotel was opened and kept the name *Metropole* for its restaurant, with its iconic yellow penguins.[141]

2-33. Metropole Hotel Turkish Bath, ca. 1912 [138]

◀ **2-34.** Hotel Metropole after addition, ca. 1924 [142]

▼

2-35. 21c Hotel Penguin and guest

The Power Building (Kennedy Power Building) was designed by Cincinnati architect *Harry Hake* and finished in 1903.[143] Ten years later, the Steinkamp brothers added two additional floors to the building for *Thomas E. Kennedy*.[144, 145] In 1910, the Steinkamps had also designed a three-story factory for Mr. Kennedy at 337 Main Street.[146] The Power Building was converted to apartments in 2002 and renamed the *Renaissance Apartments*. Located at *224 E. Eighth Street*, the former Power Building was added to the National Register of Historic Places in 1999.[147]

2-36. Kennedy Power Building, 337 Main Street, ca. 1903 [148]

2-37. Levinson's Furniture House, 313 W. Fifth Street, ca. 1914 [153]

Joseph and Bernard designed one- and three-story *oxygen plants* on *Kenyon Avenue* in the West End for the *Ohio Electrolytic Oxygen Company* in 1914.[149, 150] Kenyon Avenue was between Freeman Avenue and Baymiller Street but does not exist today. The cost of the project was first reported at $10,000 by the *Enquirer* and $65,000 was reported in *Industrial World*.

Joseph Steinkamp and Brother prepared plans and supervised construction for a four-story store for *E. J. Babbitt* to be leased by *Levinson's Furniture House* at *313 W. Fifth Street* in 1914 that cost $15,000.[151, 152] This site is now a parking lot.[153]

Although their next project was not very glamorous, in 1914 Joseph and Bernard were involved with the design of a new concrete garage behind the *Ostholthoff and Braukman* carriage plant on *Clifton Avenue, near Vine Street*, at a cost of $10,000.[154] The area had been a stabling place for streetcar horses, which were being phased out in favor of electric power. Henry Ostholthoff was the husband of Joseph and Bernard's sister, Elizabeth.

In 1915, it was reported that Joseph Steinkamp had drawn up plans for the underground subway and parking for *Government and Fountain Squares* in downtown Cincinnati. It was to extend from Vine to Main Street and have the capacity for 176 automobiles. The plan was for it to be used mainly for businesspeople and shoppers in the downtown district. Similar plans were proposed for under Garfield Place and Courthouse Square.[155, 156] However, the construction was never realized.

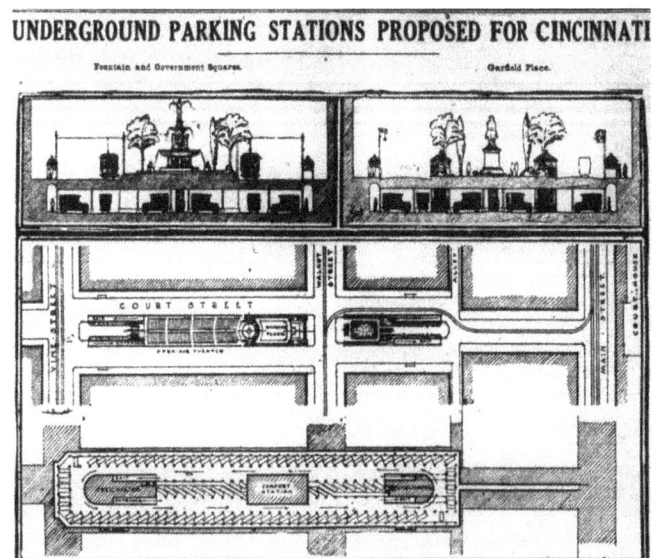

2-38. Proposed Fountain Square Underground Garage [156]

About this time, Joseph and Bernard were completing plans for a two-story and basement garage for *Frank Fox* on *E. Fifth Street* in downtown Cincinnati that was estimated to cost $30,000.[157–159]

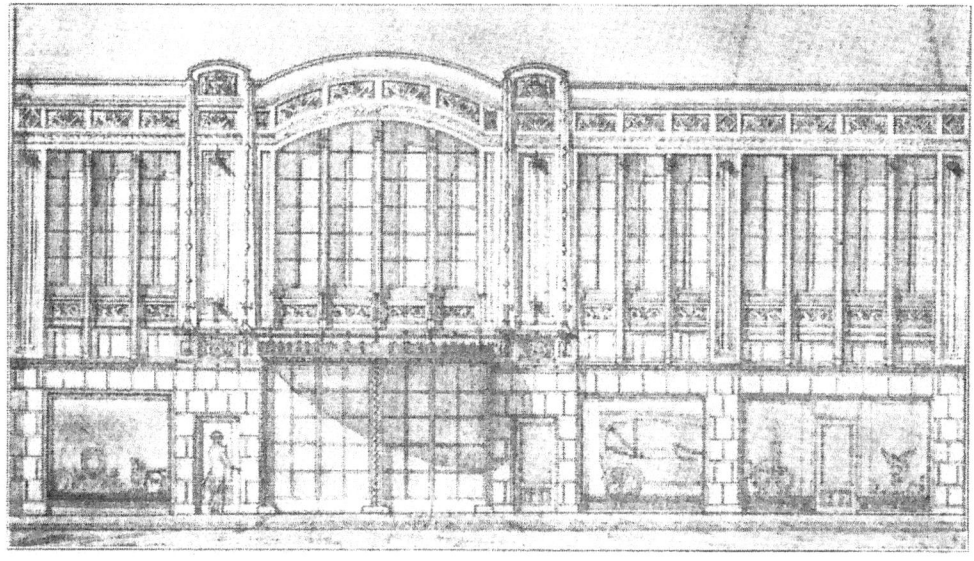

2-39. Sketch of the Fox Garage, ca. 2015 [159]

Also, in 1915, the brothers were designing yet another garage, this time on *Jackson Street* for *Towle-Cadillac Motor Company* at a cost of $10,000. The building has a distinctive "T" on the façade for Towle.[160] The building is currently the home to Know Theater of Cincinnati.[161]

2-40. Towle-Cadillac Motor Company Garage, 1120 Jackson Street, ca. 1915[162]

In 1915, Joseph and his brother designed a *two-story cold storage house* for fruit for *Joseph Castellini*, grandfather of Bob Castellini, the owner of the Cincinnati Reds baseball team, at *320 Longworth Street*. The cost of the facility was put at $10,000.[163, 164] Earlier, Longworth Street ran from Plum Street to Central Avenue through the area where the Duke Energy Center now resides.

Another garage designed by Joseph and Bernard in 1916 was for the *Wray-Chase Motor Service Company*. It was located in the West End on *Hulbert Street* and may have held up to 1,000 cars.[165,166] That same year, the company changed its name to the Chase Motor Car Company.[167]

The *Cincinnati Market Company* hired the Steinkamps to design a $250,000 two-story market house in 1917.[168] The market house was located on *Sycamore Street* between Sixth and Seventh Streets.[169] A 1917 article in the *Cincinnati Enquirer* stated, "The market building, when finished, will contain a refrigeration plant and other features necessary to make it one of the most modern in the United States."[170]

In 1917, the brothers designed a two-story service station and salesroom on the right in the photo as an addition for the ***Barlow Hodson Motor Car Company*** which was on the corner of ***Canal*** (***Central Parkway***) and ***Race Streets***.[171] The company's existing three-story building, built two years earlier, is attributed to Harry Hake. It is currently home to the Bruce D. Robertson Design Group, who restored the building.[172]

2-41. Barlow Hodson Motor Car Company, ca. **1917**[173]

2-42. Barlow Motors Building, W. Central Parkway, ca. 2020

The following year they also designed a one-story addition to a store at *318 Longworth Street* for *Mr. Castellini*, which cost $3,000.[174]

2-43. Joseph H. Kenkel Jewelry Store, 1302 Main Street, ca. 1918

The same year, they also designed an addition to the *Kenkel Jewelry Store* at *1302 Main Street*, which cost $4,000.[174] Joseph Kenkel was Joseph's neighbor on Suire Avenue.[175]

Joseph and Bernard designed a magnificent three-story commercial garage for the *Charles Schlear Motor Car Company* in 1919 that cost $45,000. It was located at the corner of *Ninth and Sycamore Streets*.[176]

2-44. Charles Schlear Motor Car Company, ca. 1919 [177]

2-45. Fox Klein Motor Car Company, 316 Reading Road, ca. 1919 [179]

2-46. Brew Dog Taproom, ca. 2021

The brothers remodeled the building at *316 Reading Road* for the *Fox Klein Motor Car Company* in 1919[b].[178] The company had its grand opening in 1921 but was sold the following year. The refurbished building is now a Brew Dog taproom.

Around the turn of the century, there were several hotels in the area near the Central Union Station (also known as the Grand Central Depot) at Third Street and Central Avenue.[180] They included the Grand Hotel[181], the *Imperial Hotel*, and the *Center Depot Palace Hotel* (also known as the Union Depot Palace Hotel, or just the Depot Palace Hotel), which was later renamed the *Plaza Hotel*.[182] In 1919 and 1921, Joseph and Bernard were reported to be designing additions and alterations to the *Union Depot Palace Hotel/Plaza Hotel* for *John J. Burckhauser and William E. Barrs*.[183, 184] The brothers were also reported to be making additions to the *Imperial Hotel* in 1920, and the owners of this hotel were again listed as John J. Burckhauser and William E. Barrs.[185] However, the owner of the Imperial Hotel was earlier listed as either *Joseph Burkhardt*[186] or *Jacob Bernhardt*[c].[187] It's not clear if the owner was incorrectly identified or whether the brothers ever worked on the Imperial Hotel.

---

[b] The notice in *The American Contractor* lists the new building for the Fox Klein Motor Car Company on Gilbert Avenue. However, they never had a business on Gilbert, and an ad for the company states that they purchased and remodeled the property at 316 Reading Road for their new business. One must assume this was the location that the Steinkamps designed for the company.

[c] The 1909 *Cincinnati Business Directory* lists Jacon Burkhardt as the proprietor of the Imperial Hotel and J. T. Burkhardt as the manager.

In addition to the *Knights of Columbus* building the brothers designed in Price Hill, they also designed one downtown at *14–18 E Ninth Street* in 1920. It was valued at $25,000.[188]

In 1920, the brothers designed a one-story building for *A. B. True* [sic] at *922 Race Street*.[189] This was most likely *August B. Trum*, a prominent Cincinnati businessman and former head of the Trum Coal Company who passed away in 1921.[190] Later that year, it was advertised for lease as an automobile showroom.[191] It is now the home of the Northside Distilling Company.

2-47. 922 Race Street, ca. 1920

The Steinkamp brothers designed a one-story *garage* for *Charles L. Shannon* at *17 E. Canal Street (Central Parkway)* in 1920.[192] Charles L. Shannon and Sons were "Importers of and Contractors for Tile and Ceramic Mosaic Work for Floors, Walls, Ceilings and Special Fire Places."[193] The Shannon Company supplied tile for many of the Emery buildings, and the Steinkamps would certainly have collaborated with them on many projects.[194] It's quite possible that the Shannon Company supplied the beautiful terrazzo floors in Joseph's home in Price Hill.

Another remodeling that year was for a loft building belonging to *The Courtland Co.*, of which Morris James Dale was the president. It was located at *725–729 Sycamore Street* and the remodeling cost $25,000.[195] It is now the site of a parking lot.

Samuel Hannaford and Sons designed the *Ohio National Guard Armory* building in the West End in 1886.[196] However, Joseph Steinkamp and Bro. were enlisted to design renovations to the building in 1927.[197] The armory was placed on the National Register of Historic Places in 1980. Unfortunately, this once magnificent building was demolished in the mid-1980s.[198]

2-48. Kennedy Loft Building, 118 E. Eighth Street, ca 1925

Working again for *Thomas E. Kennedy*, the brothers designed a six-story loft building in 1923 on *Eighth Street*.[198]

The construction of the *American Building* at *30 E. Central Parkway* appears to have had a few starts and stops. In 1923, the *Enquirer* reported the building would be 10 stories at a cost of $800,000.[199] This same article stated that the building was being proposed as the permanent home of the *American Pharmaceutical Association (APhA)*. The *Cincinnati Post* reported that the building would consist of 15 stories and would break into terraces; it put the price tag at $1,000,000.[200] The *Post* also reported that groundbreaking was scheduled for mid-October 1927 and that Joseph G. Steinkamp and Bro. had been selected as the architects for the building. It was later reported the building would be 15 stories, at a cost of $706,000, in January 1928.[201] The property on which the building was to be erected was owned by Frank H. Freericks, secretary and general counsel of the insurance company whose offices were in the Mercantile Library Building (which was designed by the Steinkamps and where they had their offices at the time). The final 17-story building gets its name from its first anchor tenant, the *American Druggists Fire Insurance Company*, which offered the APhA a floor of the new building and free heat and light.[202]

2-49. The American Building under construction, 30 E. Central Parkway, ca. 1927 [173]

When completed in 1928, the American Building was hailed as a major example of Art Deco-influenced architecture in Cincinnati. Some reports suggest its set-back upper floors and geometric motifs were designed after the Empire State Building, but the planning for that building would not begin until 1930, two years after completion of the American Building.[203] However, the building did follow New York's building code that required buildings above a certain height be terraced away from the street to permit light to reach the ground.[204] Dr. J.H. Beal (front row, far right), Chair of the Board of Directors of the American Druggists Fire Insurance Company posed in front of construction site.[206]

2-50. Board of Directors for the American Building [205]

2-51. The American Building, ca. 1929 [206]

2-52. The American Building, ca. 2020 [207]

The American was the first air-conditioned building in Cincinnati and the first west of the Alleghenies. It also had a built-in 176-car parking garage to accommodate prospective owners who were responding to the dawn of the automotive age.[208] On November 17, 1928, the American Building was dedicated with addresses by Cincinnati Vice Mayor Stanley Matthews and the President of the American Druggists Fire Insurance Company, Charles H. Avery, among other dignitaries. Mr. Freericks was master of ceremonies. During the dedication ceremonies, documents and newspapers were placed in the "Century Box" which was sealed in the walls of the edifice.[209] Of all the buildings designed by Joseph and Bernard Steinkamp, the American Building is certainly one of the most impressive.

The American Building is adorned with strange and mysterious carved figures. Two are of crouching, primitive-looking men. Following the sign of the zodiac over the archway is a "puffer," or alchemist, and a Star of David. Still others include a Zeus-like figure holding a lightning bolt, which signifies electricity, and a woman by a hearth, symbolizing heat. The top of the building is adorned with a number of unique symbols, including an eagle. Unfortunately, the city of Cincinnati was in competition with four other cities as the location of the APhA (currently the American Pharmacists Association), which eventually decided to locate in Washington, DC, in 1934.[202] In 2004, a complete renovation turned the former office building into 37 luxury condominiums, topped off by a three-level penthouse.[212]

2-53. Primitive-looking man

2-54. Primitive-looking man

2-55. Puffer [210]

2-56. Decorative symbols on the top of the American Building [211]

Rebounding from the Depression, the Steinkamp brothers' business was taking an upswing at the end of the 1930s. In March 1937, *Hudepohl Brewing Company* applied for a permit to build a two-story refrigeration storage building at *809 West Sixth Street*. Steinkamp, Gillespie, and Felsberg were listed as the architects.[213] The following month, Hudepohl Brewing Company obtained a contract for a new shipping and office building at *38 E. McMicken Avenue*. The award was made through Joseph G. and Bernard F. Steinkamp, C.H. Gillespie, and Nelson Felsberg in the amount of $30,000.[214] The building now houses the McMicken Health Collaborative. In 1939, Felsberg and Gillespie designed a three-story bottling unit for the brewery at the Sixth Street location.[215] Nelson Felsberg went on to work on 12 more buildings for the Hudepohl Brewing Company.[4]

2-57. Hudepohl Brewing Company, Bottling Department, 38 E. McMicken Avenue, ca. 1937

2-59. Decorative column on the Red Fox Grill, 232 E. Sixth Street, ca. 1937

2-58. Lintel at former Hudepohl building on Sixth Street

Also, in 1937, the *Cincinnati Enquirer* reported that two buildings owned by *Xavier University* on *E. Sixth Street* were being razed to make room for a one-story store to be designed by Joseph and Bernard.[216] That location now houses the *Red Fox Grill*. The detail work on the columns of the building certainly appears to be in a style used by the brothers in other buildings.

The same year, the brothers and their partners remodeled a building at *209–211 E. Third Street* for *Mrs. Georgianna Schoolfield* of Charleston, WV.[217]

The firm also worked on a complete rehabilitation of a building next door at *213–219 E. Third Street* for *Dr. H. H. Young* of Robertsburg, WV.[218, 219] Mrs. Schoolfield was married to

Dr. G. C. Schoolfield, and Dr. Harry Young was her brother.[220] Both of these buildings have since been replaced by high-rises.

The Steinkamp brothers, along with partners Gillespie and Felsberg, designed a new home for the *Consolidated Trucking Company* at the intersection of *Flint, Haefer, and Courtland (Cortlandt) Streets* in 1937.[221]

2-60. Sketch of the Consolidated Trucking Company, ca. 1937 [221]

In what may have been their last collaborations downtown, Joseph and Bernard designed a 20-door loading dock for the *Dixie-Ohio Express Company* at *Flint Street and Dalton Avenue* in 1939.[222]

CHAPTER 3

Xavier University Campus

Among the most impressive works by Joseph and Bernard are the magnificent, castle-like structures they designed for Xavier University in Avondale. Around 1913, the brothers began a 15-year collaboration with Xavier that culminated in seven structures on the North Avondale campus. The brothers were very familiar with St. Xavier College, as both had attended the school at one time and their brother George had graduated from Xavier in 1904. They had also drawn up plans for renovations of the college's Sycamore Street building in 1910.[1, 2] In 1911, the college purchased the Avondale Athletic Club property in North Avondale for $87,000, with the intent that it would eventually be used for the new campus.[3]

When St. Xavier College moved from the Sycamore Street location to its current site in North Avondale in 1912, it needed buildings to house its classes. While school operated in the Union Building (formally the clubhouse for the Avondale Athletic Club), the college raised funds for the new construction. By the following year, its alumni association had commissioned Joseph G. Steinkamp and Brother to draw up long-range plans for development of the new campus.[4]

It appears that Joseph and Bernard started drawing up plans for the Xavier campus buildings in 1915 and 1916, to cost an estimated $200,000[5-9] By the following year, the cost of the buildings had risen to $350,000.[10] According to Fortin, "The architectural firm of Joseph G. Steinkamp and Brother drew up plans for the new buildings on the campus. The first set of plans for the east side of the campus between Northside and Herald Avenues called for a faculty building, student dormitory, and classroom building; for the west side between Northside and Dana and Winding Way the plans included the former clubhouse, a gymnasium and outdoor swimming pool, tennis courts, basketball courts, handball courts, football and baseball fields, and an oval running track."[11] They eventually were responsible for the design of five of the earliest buildings on the Xavier campus (*Hinkle Hall*, *Edgecliff Hall*, *Elet Hall*, *Albers Hall*, and *Schmidt Hall*), plus the *Field House and Gymnasium* and the now-demolished *Xavier Football Stadium*. The five castle-like structures in the Tudor style, highlighted by medieval elements such as octagonal towers, sit above Victory Parkway to the west and resemble a single fortress.[12] In addition to the plans for the original school buildings, the Steinkamps also submitted a supplemental set of plans that included a chapel, a research laboratory for the graduate department, an arboretum, and an open-air theater. However, those plans were never implemented.[13]

In the middle of this fortress is *Hinkle Hall* (1919), dedicated in 1920 and named after Mrs. Frederick W. (Susanna) Hinkle, a benefactor of the university. This structure served as the residence hall for the Jesuit faculty.[14] The three-story Hinkle Hall, Tudor-Gothic in design, was built at a cost of $160,000.[15] Its turrets are said to be modeled after the Francis Xavier family castle in Navarre, Spain.[16]

3-1. Early construction photo of Hinkle Hall, ca. 1920 [17]

3-2. Hinkle Hall, ca. 2020 [17]

3-3. Francis Xavier Family Castle [18]

Edgecliff Hall, originally *Alumni Science Hall* (1919), was renamed after the former Edgecliff College and cost $50,000. It is now home to the Department of Music.[19, 20]

3-4. Edgecliff Hall, ca. 1919 [21]

When classes began in September 1924, St. Xavier College became a boarding college for the first time since 1854. *Elet Hall*, built in 1924 and named after Father John Elet, the first Jesuit president of Xavier University, accommodated 90 resident students.[22, 23] Because of the new dormitory, enrollment that year rose by 65 students to a total of 249.

3-5. Elet Hall, ca. 1924 [21]

Schmidt Hall (1926) housed the university's first library but now serves as the administration building. It is named after Walter S. Schmidt, a member of the class of 1905 and a benefactor of Xavier University. The Xavier College Foundation raised $135,000 for its construction.[24]

3-6. Schmidt Hall, ca. 1926 [17]

The March 24, 1926, issue of the *Xaverian* posted the front-page headline "Donation of $200,000 will give St. Xavier gymnasium." The donation, made possible by the efforts of Walter S. Schmidt, had been announced about a week earlier by St. Xavier's president, Rev. Hubert F. Brockman, S.J., at the annual banquet of the Business Men's Club.[25] The Engineering firm of Lieberman and Hein of Chicago would manage the project but Joseph G. Steinkamp and Brother would draw the plans for the gymnasium. *The Catholic Telegraph* reported that the new gymnasium would seat 12,500, which was rather unrealistic.[26] The seating capacity had also been reported to be only 5,000.[27] However, the new field house was not welcomed by all. The neighbor residents protested the erection of the field house, claiming that it would destroy the privacy of the district because of the traffic and noise. The Acting Commissioner of Buildings, George Schmid, stated that there was nothing in the zoning law that would prevent issuance of the building permit for the field house.[28]

3-7. Schmidt Field House, ca. 1927

The total cost of the *St. Xavier Gymnasium* (later renamed the *Schmidt Memorial Fieldhouse*) was reported to be $250,000, although other estimates were as high as $325,000.[29] The fieldhouse is actually dedicated to Walter Schmidt's parents, Mrs. Appoline Tetedoux and Frederick A. Schmidt.[30]

When opened in 1928, the gymnasium had the largest seating capacity of any structure in Cincinnati[26] and "...will be in harmony with the present campus structures, which are of Gothic type."[25] However, it was also noted that the Steinkamps "successfully mingled medieval elements, such as octagonal towers, with accents in the Tudor style."[25] Construction took place in 1927, and the gymnasium's opening on March 7, 1928, was inaugurated with a come-from-behind win against basketball archrival the University of Cincinnati, before almost 10,000 roaring fans.[31]

In 1927, Knute Rockne, the legendary University of Notre Dame football coach, opened a campaign dinner at the Sinton Hotel to raise funds for a new football stadium for the Xavier campus.[32] In February 1928, Joseph and Bernard applied for a modification of the building code for the *Xavier Football Stadium*.[33] With the help of a fundraising drive led by Myers Y. Cooper, later governor of Ohio, the $300,000, 15,000-seat Corcoran Stadium officially opened at Homecoming on Nov. 23, 1929. According to a handwritten note in the University Archives, the stadium offered "a splendid view for all."[29, 34]

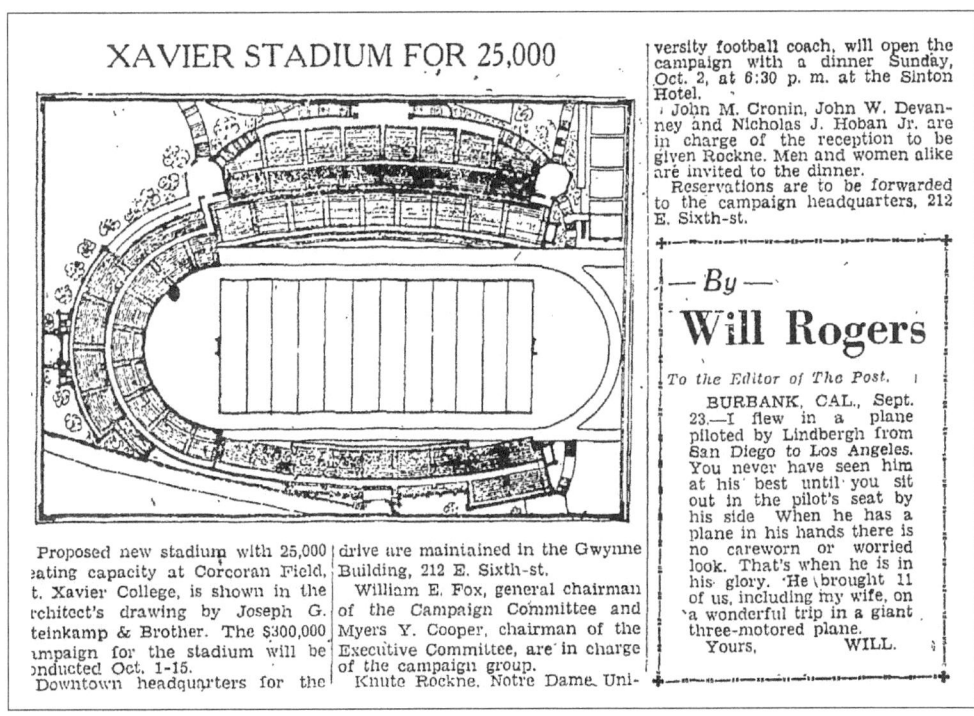

3-8. Plans for Football Stadium [32]

Corcoran Stadium is named in honor of John and E.B. Corcoran. The Corcorans were "generous local contributors to the stadium fund."[35] Dr. A. A. Shaw, President of Denison University, was a special guest at the dedication ceremonies.[36] Corcoran Stadium hosted the Xavier University Musketeers football team until the school dropped the football program for financial reasons in 1973. The stadium was finally razed in 1988, after attempts to revive the football program in Division III failed.

Corcoran Stadium can be seen in the 1946 movie *The Best Years of Our Lives* as "Jackson High Football Stadium."[37] The stadium also played host to one NFL game, on October 7, 1934, when the Cincinnati Reds took on the Chicago Cardinals. The Reds lost the game by a score of 13–0, before 2,500 Reds fans.[38]

3-9. Corcoran Stadium, ca. 1929

The headline in the *Cincinnati Enquirer* read, "College to Expand with Biology Building" in its March 5th, 1929 edition. St. Xavier College President, Rev. Hubert F. Brockman, S. J., announced that another step in the expansion of the campus was about to start with the construction of the new **Biology Building**. As with many of the other recently completed buildings on campus, it was being designed by Joseph G. Steinkamp and Bro. and built by Leibold-Farrell Construction Company. It was reported the new building would be north of Hinkle Hall and connected to it with an enclosed corridor. With the completion of the Biology Building, in addition to the other recently completed buildings, it was expected that the school's enrollment would soon reach 1000 students.[40, 41]

The Xavier Biology Building (now **Albers Hall**) was built at a cost of $120,000 to $150,000 with the aid of a gift from former State Senator Robert J. O'Brien.[29, 40–42] It is three stories in height and was built in the Tudor Gothic style to harmonize with the other buildings of the campus group.

It also housed the offices of the president and the director of public relations. In addition to classrooms and laboratories, the building had a main lecture room that seated 150. It was dedicated in 1929 and is still a classroom building.

3-10. Plans for the Biology Building, Albers Hall [41]

3-11. Albers Hall, ca. 1929 [21]

CHAPTER 4

Avondale and North Avondale

In 1895, Daniel J. Kenny described Avondale as "one of the most beautiful and picturesque suburbs of the city."[1] He added that it was "for years the home of many of the most prominent merchants and manufacturers of Cincinnati." By the end of the twentieth century, electric trolleys allowed businesses to move from the restrictions of the basin to the suburbs. As Stradling pointed out, "Streets with trolley lines developed more intensely than those without, as business districts and apartment buildings thrived on the easy access provided by the streetcars."[2] Thomas Emery's Sons, along with Joseph and Bernard Steinkamp, would play an important role in further developing many high-end luxury apartments in Avondale, especially along Reading Road. These buildings became known as "Streetcar Suburb Apartment Buildings" because of their access to this mode of transportation.[3]

That same year, *Thomas J. and J. J. Emery* donated $35,000 towards the construction of a *Colored Orphan Asylum* in Avondale.[4,5] It was located at *Melish Avenue and Emery* (renamed Van Buren) Avenue; I-71 now runs through this site.[6] At the building's dedication the following November, an oration was given by Professor Booker T. Washington.[7] Although Joseph was working with the Emery family at this time, he was not credited with the building's design. However, in 1919 Joseph and Bernard were developing plans for a two-story addition to the asylum, to cost $25,000.[8] In various issues of *The American Contractor*, it was listed as being located on "Webyman," "Wehyman," or "Wayman" Avenue. It was probably on Wehrman Avenue, which is near the location of the 1886 building.[8] However, the *Williams' Cincinnati Directory* for 1920 indicated that the address for the Colored Orphan Asylum was Melish and Van Buren.[9]

4-1. Colored Orphan Asylum, ca. 1895[5]

The *Cumberland* was built for *Thomas Emery's Sons* at the corner of *Reading Road and Cleveland Avenue* in 1896. Along with the Somerset, this was one of the family's earliest endeavors in Avondale and featured a unique, dumbbell-shaped plan with six flats. The Cumberland was located across the street from Haddon Hall.[10] At one time it was clad in aluminum siding.[11] However, some of the detail of the original building may be seen above the siding in the photo below. Now there is only a vacant lot where it once stood.

4-2. 808 Cleveland Avenue. The Cumberland, ca. 1896 [12]

The *Somerset* was the first large-scale apartment built in the Cincinnati neighborhood of Avondale and was completed in 1896, the same year that Avondale was annexed to the city.[11] It was a four-story building containing 24 units at *Reading Road and Blair Avenue*. Designed by the Steinkamps and built by *Thomas Emery's Sons*, it reflects the Queen Anne style with Renaissance Revival elements. The Somerset is an example of the "Streetcar Suburb Apartment Building" and was one of several upper- and middle-class apartments built along Reading Road, a major streetcar artery which was electrified around 1890. Around this time, many upwardly mobile Jewish professionals relocated to the Avondale neighborhood to escape the crowding and pollution in the city. The Emery family owned the Somerset until 1942, and the next mortgage holder eventually defaulted to Fannie Mae in 2011. The Community Builders purchased it from Fannie Mae in 2012. Somerset Manor on Blair Avenue is part of a $29.5 million federal grant-funded redevelopment project in Avondale.[13] It was placed on the National Register of Historic Places in 2014.[14]

In 1899, Joseph and Bernard designed the *North and South Warwick Apartments* in Avondale.[10, 16] They were located at *Blair Avenue and Reading Road* and are no long standing. The North Warwick was heavily damaged in a fatal fire in 1967 and later that same year was destroyed by arsonists during the riots and eventually torn down.[17] The South Warwick was also damaged in a fire in 1999, and it too was finally demolished.[18]

4-3. The Somerset, ca. 1896 [15]

4-4. North Warwick, ca. 1899 [16]

4-5. South Warwick ca. 1899 [16]

In 1901, the Steinkamps designed The *Waldemar Apartments* on the corner of *Reading Road and Hickman Avenue.*[10, 19] It appears that they were demolished in 1926 or 1927.[20]

Haddon Hall, most likely built around 1900/1901, was another large high-end apartment complex built by *Thomas Emery's Sons*.[21] The four-story complex was built in the Dutch Colonial Revival Style on *Reading Road* and features a single ground-floor entrance with a large portico.[16, 22]

According to *The Bicentennial Guide to Greater Cincinnati: A Portrait of Two Hundred Years*, "Haddon Hall Apartments, 3814 Reading Road, is one of the earlier, large apartment buildings put up to provide attractive housing … near public transportation and the center of the suburban neighborhood. Erected around 1900 by the Emery family, the massive 4-story gambrel roofed structure was designed by Joseph Steinkamp… to blend with Avondale's mansions."[23] Cincinnati Mayor John Cranley and other city officials joined Wallick Communities to cut the ribbon and mark the restoration of the iconic Haddon Hall Apartments. It was placed on the National Register of Historic Places in 1982.[24]

4-6. Haddon Hall, ca. 1902 [25]

Over the years, the brothers designed homes for many of the businessmen who had their offices in the Mercantile Library Building. One of the first was a flat for *Nicholas P. Smith*, of Nicholas P. Smith & Co., Auctioneers, Loans, and Investments in 1904. It was located at *3437 Wilson Avenue*.[26, 27]

Also, in 1904, the brothers designed a St. Louis flat for *Mr. Ben B. Dale,* Attorney, on *Reading Road, near Ridgeway Avenue* to cost $10,000.[28]

In 1909, two articles were published that highlighted many of the Steinkamp-designed apartments from the turn of the century. One was by Walter Maxwell in *Saxby's Magazine*[6] and the second was in the *Ohio Architect and Builder*.[29] The focus of the Maxwell article was on the Emery family, and the other article highlighted recent building construction in Cincinnati. Neither article really mentioned the brothers, but both included photos of the two distinguished looking gentlemen in profile. Some Steinkamp designs in Avondale were shown in both articles, but there was some confusion as to the names of some of the apartments.[a]

---

[a] The *Ohio Architect and Builder* included a photo of an apartment that it called "*The Barcelona*," but the Maxwell article called the same building "*The Madrid*." Extensive searches for the Barcelona Apartments or Flats did not turn up a building with that name. Also, both articles show the same building as "*The Madrid*" and "*The Granada*" apartments.

Joseph and Bernard were credited with five more apartments built for *Thomas Emery's Sons* in Avondale. The two articles included *The Granada* and *The Madrid* (1905), and *The Aragon* and *The Castile* (1906).[16, 29] The four apartments were near each other on *Burnet Avenue*, now the site of the Cincinnati Children's Hospital.

4-7. The Madrid, ca. 1905 [30]

Although *The Essex* (1903) was not included in either of the two articles, it was another one of the apartments built in Avondale by the *Emerys* in the early part of the 20th century. The building, with six flats on each of four stories, was on the corner of *Reading Road and Cleveland Avenue*. It was demolished in 1983.[31, 32]

4-8. The Essex Apartments, ca. 1909 [32]

4-9. The Aragon and Castile, ca. 1909 [30]

4-10. The Granada, ca. 1909 [33]

Joseph and Bernard designed a three-story apartment that cost $15,000 in 1908 for *Dr. A. Strashun*, a physician and surgeon who owned Strashun's Pharmacy, at the corner of *Burnet and Erkenbrecher (Albany) Avenues*.[34–36]

About this time, the Steinkamp brothers drew up plans for a three and one-half story apartment for *Clarence E. Schaffner* on *Maple Avenue* in Avondale, known as

4-11. 615 Maple Avenue. The Schaffner, ca. 1907 [38]

The Schaffner.[37, 38] After years of neglect, the building has been restored to its former style. This project marked the beginning of the brothers' collaboration with Schaffner, which later included the Georgian Terrace Apartments on Madison Road and Schaffner's home nearby on Observatory Road, near Madison.

4-12. The Schaffner, ca. 2014 [39]

Built in 1908, *Poinciana Flats* is a large Streetcar Suburb Apartment Building in South Avondale with 44 apartments, designed by Joseph and Bernard along *Reading Road*. Consisting of four stories in the Queen Anne style with Romanesque Revival architectural details, it features an irregular U-shaped design with a deep, narrow

4-13. Poinciana Flats, 3522 Reading Road, ca. 1908 [42]

courtyard. The Poinciana is thought to be the third apartment building constructed by the ***Krug Realty Company***. This is the largest of the three apartment buildings, which suggests that the other two were successful investments.[40] In 1967 the Krug Realty Company sold the Poinciana, and it changed hands several times before being purchased by the current owners in 2012. It was placed on the National Register of Historic Places in 2014.[41] Currently, all 44 apartments are Section 8 assisted living units. There is no information as to why it was named after the tropical flowering Poinciana tree.

Also, in 1908, the brothers designed an apartment for ***Sanson M. Cooper*** on ***Rockdale Avenue*** that would expand the original building plans to 108 rooms and cost $85,000.[43, 44] It contained 24 suites of five or six rooms with quarters for domestic help as part of each apartment. It was across from Knox (Knott) Street and was named "Virginia" after Mr. Cooper's daughter. Sanson Cooper was the brother of Myers Y. Cooper, the 51st Governor of Ohio, for whom the Steinkamps probably designed the Cooper Apartments in Walnut Hills in 1928. It is still in use today, but in need of renovation.

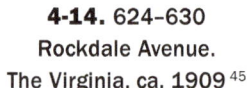
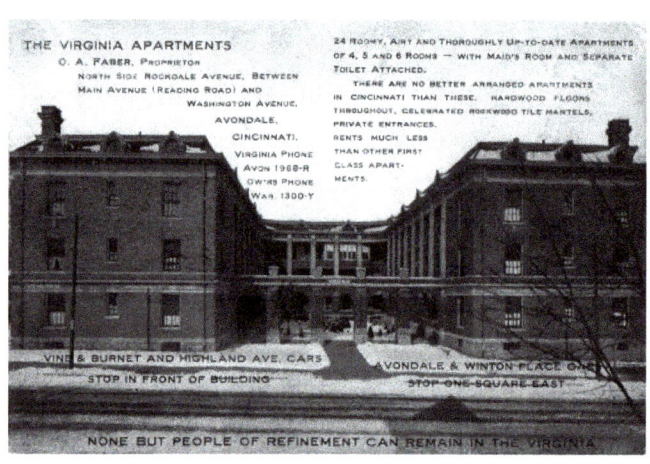

4-14. 624–630 Rockdale Avenue. The Virginia, ca. 1909 [45]

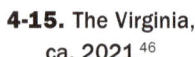

4-15. The Virginia, ca. 2021 [46]

Continuing their work in 1908, Joseph and Bernard designed either a three- or four-story apartment at ***576 Hale Avenue*** near Reading Road at a cost of either $30,000,

$40,000 or $75,000, depending on several reports. *Mr. Morris Strauss* was president of the French Benzol Dry Cleaning Company in Walnut Hills, for whom the Steinkamps worked around this time.[47-49] The building was demolished sometime after 2014.

4-16. The Hale Apartments, ca. 1908 [50]

Several Cincinnati dry cleaners established the *Cincinnati Dry Cleaning Company* in 1909 to protect the rights of 350 individual tailors, dyers, and cleaners, with plans to construct a huge facility on *Emery Avenue (later Van Buren)*, between Shillito and Whittier Streets and opposite the Colored Orphans Asylum. Joseph and Bernard were listed as the architects for the new building.[51, 52] However, the following year, it was reported that the brothers were designing a "modest plant" for the dry-cleaning company that was directly opposite the original site that cost $8000.[53, 54]

The Steinkamps designed two duplex buildings for *Nicholas P. Smith*, of Nicholas P. Smith & Co., who were real estate brokers, dealers, and appraisers, in 1909. They were located at the corner of *Hickory and Harvey Avenues* and cost $17,000.[55]

The Crescent (ca. 1911) was built by *Val Duttenhofer, Jr.*, owner of Val Duttenhofer Company, one of the largest manufacturers of ladies' shoes in Cincinnati.[56] However, the architect for this apartment building, which was labelled "…Avondale's most exclusive apartment house…," is not known.[57] The building certainly looks like it could be a Steinkamp design and was in the same location where they were designing several large apartment buildings for Thomas Emery's Sons. The National Register of Historic Places

4-17. The Crescent, ca. 1911 [45]

Registration Form compares the Crescent to Haddon Hall, The Alexandra, and the Verona, all Court Apartment Buildings designed by the Steinkamps and built by the Emerys.[58] The Duttenhofer family kept ownership of the Crescent until 1959, and the apartment building was placed on the National Register of Historic Places in 2014.[59]

In 1913, the Steinkamps designed a two-story house on *Albany (now Erkenbrecher) Avenue* near Vine Street for *Charles Schmidt*.[60, 61] However, only a parking lot sits where the house was once located.

Joseph and Bernard developed plans for the *St. Andrew's Parochial School* on *Blair Avenue and Reading Road* in 1922.[62, 63] The original school and its replacement were near several Steinkamp designs, including Haddon Hall, the Schaffner, and the Somerset. On May 3, 1925, the cornerstone of the school was placed with Monsignor Louis J. Nau officiating[64], and the school was dedicated in September of the same year.[65] Because of declining enrollment, the school closed in 1965.[66]

In 1923, *C. P. Morton of* Dana Avenue hired the brothers to design a one-story stucco garage at *3864 Reading Road* at a cost of $2,700.[67]

After the Steinkamp brothers sought a modification to the building code in 1935 to build a one-story store on the corner of *Burnet and Northern Avenues* for *J.O. Frank*, they received a contract from the *Franklin Realty Company* to design a group of five stores at this location. Each store was to have a "bulkhead of black structural glass and a continuous awning hood above, running the length of the five stores."[68–71] The picture in the photo may or may not be the correct building, but it certainly matches the description. The building was demolished around 2010. This location was the site of *Pilder's Food Market*, and a city directory notes that Charles Pilder was located at this address in 1937.[71]

4-18. Block of stores, Burnet and Northern Avenues, ca. 1936 [72]

CHAPTER 5

Walnut Hills and East Walnut Hills

The Steinkamps—initially Johann alone, then Johann with Joseph, and later Joseph with brother Bernard—designed many structures in Walnut Hills and East Walnut Hills, during the period from the 1890s to around 1930. It was reported that the Emerys built 22 brick homes in Walnut Hills just before the turn of the century. Since the Steinkamp family served as the primary architects for the Emerys, they must have contributed to the design of most of them. Along McMillan Street, they designed at least six large apartment buildings, primarily for Thomas Emery's Sons, along with the chapel and addition to St. Ursula Academy. On Grand Avenue (later Sinton), they designed the Eden on the south end, at least seven homes on Sinton, and the Mason Towle Company Dodge dealership on the corner of Sinton and Gilbert Avenue. They also renovated the Emerys' property on the opposite corner of Sinton and Gilbert and were reported to have designed a large dry-cleaning plant across Gilbert, opposite Sinton.

In what appears to be the Steinkamps' earliest projects in Walnut Hills, Johann designed several homes located on *Sinton (Grand) Avenue* in Walnut Hills. He was reported to have designed first one ($10,000), then four ($20,000), and finally seven ($40,000) frame and brick buildings in 1889.[1-3] Several single-family homes on Sinton Avenue were built around this time period, making it difficult to pinpoint the exact locations.

Working just after his father's death, Joseph designed a two-story home on *Klein Street* for *Joseph H. Boose* in 1892 that cost $3,000.[4]

Shortly afterward, Joseph designed a two and one-half story flat at the corner of *Gilbert Avenue and Grand (Sinton) Avenue* in 1894 for *Thomas Emery's Sons* at a cost of $3,200.[5]

5-1. Emery Flat, 2220 Gilbert Avenue, ca. 1894

In 1894, Joseph designed a three and one-half story addition to the *Little Sisters of the Poor Home for the Aged* at a cost of $3,000.[6, 7] It was located on *Montgomery Road opposite Symmes Street.*

Toward the end of *Sinton Avenue*, *Eden Flats* was one of the largest and most striking of the early, central corridor walk-up apartments. Designed by Joseph in 1894 for *Thomas Emery's Sons*, the four-story Richardsonian Romanesque building with an ashlar sandstone façade was in the Gilbert-Sinton Historic District.[8, 9]

5-2. Eden Flats, 2106 Sinton Avenue, ca. 1895 [10]

5-3. Eden Flats, ca. 2020

The Steinkamp brothers are often given credit for designing the Gilbert *Emery Row Apartments* on *Gilbert Avenue* for *Thomas Emery's Sons*. However, Bernard had not started working with Joseph in 1889 and J.B. was still working at this time. This group of historic row houses, composed of six individual small houses and a larger commercial building with a cast iron front, was constructed in the Queen Anne style. This was an unusual construction style for row houses in Cincinnati.[11] In 1982, like many of the Steinkamp/Emery apartment buildings, it was placed on the National Register of Historic Places.[12]

5-4. Gilbert Row Apartments, 2152–2156 Gilbert Avenue, ca. 1889 [13]

At *McMillan Street and Kemper Lane*, Joseph and Bernard designed the *Nelson Apartments* in 1900.[14] The Nelson was at the northwest corner of McMillan and Kemper, located where the former Kroger store was located. Along with the Kinsey Flats and Melbourne Flats, the Nelson is an example of designs on a smaller scale by the Steinkamps. Later, in 1907, they designed the Guarantee Realty Company property across the street from the Nelson.

5-5. Nelson Apartments, ca. 1900 [15]

After 1900, the firm of Joseph Steinkamp and Brother began a period in which they constructed a number of large, modern apartment complexes in the Clifton, Avondale, and Walnut Hills areas of Cincinnati. The first of these large complexes was the *Alexandra,* on the corner of *E. William Howard Taft and Gilbert Avenue* (ca. 1904). The 54-unit building, the largest apartment complex in the city at that time, was developed by *Thomas Emery's Sons* and was named after John's daughter Alexandra Moore. It was built in the American Colonial Revival style and represented "an artistic protest" according to architectural historian Walter Langsam. He also stated, "The styling enables the building to utilize land economically and blend in with a very fashionable neighborhood."[16] In 1993 much of the structure was destroyed by fire, and it was subsequently condemned. The apartment building reopened in 2003 after undergoing a $12.7 million renovation and now provides 83 affordable apartments for senior citizens. The newly renovated 100-year-old Alexandra apartment complex was awarded the 2004 Paragon Award for the best garden/townhouse pre-dating 1979. The award is the highest honor bestowed by the National Apartment Association.[17] It was placed on the National Register of Historic Places in 1997.[18]

5-6. The Alexandra, 921 William Howard Taft Road, ca. 1904 [19]

5-7. The Alexandra, ca. 1921

In 1904, *The Western Architect and Builder* reported that the Steinkamps were designing three, two and one-half story brick and stone dwellings on the southeast corner of *Forest (now William Howard Taft Road) and Moorman Avenues* in East Walnut Hills for *A. L. Pachoud* at a cost of $2000 each.[20] Mr. Pachoud was a builder and real estate agent who had his office in the Mercantile Library and the brothers went on to collaborate on the design other buildings for him over the years. In 1904, Sanford Insurance Maps showed three lots at this location, but later they had been divided into four lots. It is possible Mr. Pachoud added an additional building using the Steinkamp's design.[21]

5-8. 2554 Moorman Avenue, ca. 1904 [22]

5-9. 2556 Moorman Avenue, ca. 1904 [23]

5-10. 2558 Moorman Avenue, ca. 1904 [24]

5-11. 2560 Moorman Avenue, ca. 1904

Also, in 1904, the brothers were making plans to remodel the *Peabody Homestead* in the *Lane Seminary* into an apartment building on Gilbert Avenue.[25–27] The remodeling was estimated to cost $5,500.[28] The building later was demolished and is now the site of Thompson MacConnell Cadillac.

Still in 1904, the brothers designed a two and one-half story residence on the west side of *Gilbert Avenue* opposite Deerfield Place for *Frank H. Batsche* at a cost of $2,500.[29]

The Navarre, another large apartment complex in Walnut Hills designed by the brothers for *Thomas Emery's Sons* in 1905, was located on *Gilbert Avenue across from Yale Avenue*. It was three and one-half stories, with 36 flats containing three to six rooms each. The estimated cost of the project was $100,000.[30, 31]

5-12. The Navarre apartment complex, 2651 Gilbert Avenue, ca. 1905

5-13. Detail of The Navarre entrance

The Steinkamp brothers designed *The Clermont*, which was built as a luxury apartment building in 1906 on *E. McMillan Street*.[32] Warminski described the tenants of the Clermont as "…generally young married couples without children and older retired people, both types attracted to the convenience this kind of living offered."[33]

5-14. The Clermont apartments, 1404–1406 E. McMillan Street, ca. 1906 [34]

5-15. Advertisement for Clermont Apartments [35]

The Verona was developed by the *Emery Sons,* and Joseph and Bernard Steinkamp were the architects. It was built in 1906 on *Park Avenue* as country apartments for wealthy Cincinnatians who lived downtown.[36] It was placed on the National Register of Historic Places in 2008.[37]

5-16. The Verona, 2356 Park Avenue, ca. 1906 [38]

5-17. The Verona

5-18. Plaque on Verona

Different from other large apartment buildings constructed at this time, the complex at the corner of *McMillan Street and Kemper Lane* appears not to have been named. It sits across from the Ransley Apartments, designed by Samuel Hannaford, and the now-demolished Nelson Apartments. In addition to apartments, the building contained a café and a garage. The 54-apartment, 203-room building was designed in 1907 for the *Guaranty Realty Company*, which was formed by several businessmen, including *Joseph G. Steinkamp and Joseph T. Carew*. The reported cost was $200,000.[39-42]

5-19. Apartment complex at McMillan Street and Kemper Lane, ca. 1907

Joseph and Bernard designed a two and one-half story home for *Louis Rechtin* on *E. McMillan Street* in E. Walnut Hills in 1908.[43] Mr. Rechtin was president of the Louis E. Rechtin & Bro. Wood Working Machinery Company[44] and in 1907, the brothers had designed a two-story addition to the Cordesman-Rechtin Company at 215 Butler Street.[45]

In 1909, Joseph and Bernard designed a house for *Charles F. Barrett*, an agent for the Adams Express Company, at *3045 Gilbert Avenue*.[46] However, by 1930, the house was no longer standing.[47]

5-20. Louis Rechtin home
1725 E. McMillian Street,
ca. 1908

When the *Home for Incurables* was expanding its Walnut Hills facility in 1909, Joseph and Bernard drew up plans for a three-story addition to the rear of the building, on *Kemper Lane*.[48]

5-21. Home for Incurables, ca. 1909 [49]

Also, in 1909, the brothers designed a "modern six-room bungalow" to be built for *M. J. Sullivan*, President of the Sullivan Printing Company, on *Myrtle Street* in East Walnut Hills.[50]

5-22. Sullivan home at 1387 Myrtle Street, ca. 1909 [51]

In 1908, Joseph and Bernard were designing a two-story stable and wagon shed on *Florence Avenue and Concord Street* for the *French Benzol Dry Cleaning Company*.[52] In 1909 and 1911, stories in the *Cincinnati Enquirer* described plans to build "a mammoth dry-cleaning plant in a central location." It was to be in Walnut Hills on *Gilbert Avenue*. The French Benzol Dry Cleaning Company, in partnership with two other local dry-cleaning companies, proposed that the plant would be "one of the show places of the city" and would include stables and a garage which were on Florence Avenue near Concord Street.[53, 54]

In 1913, an ad in the *Enquirer* places the French Benzol dry-cleaning plant at 2242–2245 Gilbert Avenue, although some ads have it located at 2243 to 2249.[55] Later, in 1919, the Sehn-Benzol-Wuerdeman Dry Cleaning Company was located at this address.[56] This location in Walnut Hills is the site of the *Gilbert Avenue Cable House,* which hauled cable cars up Gilbert Avenue from 1885 until 1898, when it was converted to electric.[57] The building was renovated several years ago to reflect the original Cable House and now is home to several businesses.

5-23. Sketch of original French Benzol Dry Cleaning Company [58]

5-24. Ad for French Benzol Dry Cleaning Company [56]

5-25. French Benzol Dry Cleaning Company, Gilbert Avenue, ca. 1913 [59]

5-26. Renovated Cable House on Gilbert Avenue, ca. 2019 [60]

Mrs. Mary Fox commissioned the Steinkamps to design a store and flats at the corner of *Gilbert Avenue and Curtis Street* in 1912. Her husband's hardware business occupied the first floor of the building, which cost $23,000.[61, 62] In 2020 the building was undergoing renovation.

5-27. Fox Hardware Store and Flat at 2436 Gilbert Avenue, ca. 1912 [63]

The brothers designed a two-story duplex for *Henry Roos*, general manager for Roos Bros, Engineers and Contractors, in 1913 for a cost of $13,500.[64] The building was constructed on *Lincoln Avenue near Winslow Street*, which is now the location of a portion of I-71. Two years later, they designed a two-story home for *Mr. Roos* on *Lincoln Avenue, near Melrose Street*, that cost $7000.[65] In 1916, it was reported that the brothers were designing a duplex on *Lincoln Avenue near Montrose Street* for *Mrs. A. E. Ross [sic]* at a cost of $6,500.[66] However, the address given for Mrs. Ross is the same as that for the Roos family.[67]

Following their conversion to the Catholic faith, *Bellamy Storer* and his wife, *Maria Longworth Storer*, the founder of Rookwood Pottery Company, were living in an apartment at *St. Ursula Academy* on *McMillan Street* in Walnut Hills. Bellamy asked his architect to design a new chapel for them to attend mass. However, the design

5-28. Chapel in St. Ursula Academy, ca. 1914

turned out to be very costly. The Ursuline Sisters purchased the Worchester and Harrison homes on E. McMillan Street in 1910. In 1914 Mother Fidelis Coleman asked *Sister Mary Carmel McLellan* to sketch a design for the chapel. Following her sketch, Joseph Steinkamp was hired, and plans were drawn up in the Baroque/Romanesque style for the chapel that connected the Worchester and Harrison houses. Living quarters for Bellamy and Maria L. Storer were added to the rear of the Harrison house.[68–73] Maria and Bellamy donated $10,000 towards the construction of the chapel. The cornerstone for the chapel was laid in August of 1915 and the chapel was dedicated on May 31, 1916 by Archbishop Moeller.[68]

The brothers designed a home for *Frank Sawyer* in 1917 at the corner of *McMillan and Stanton Avenues* at a cost of $6,000.[74] This building has been demolished to make room for new construction.

Also, in 1917, they designed the *Garonne*, a three-story apartment building of eight suites for *Thomas Emery's Sons* at the corner of *Oak Street and Gilbert Avenue*.[75, 76] In 1944, the Thomas J. Emery Memorial sold the Navarre and the Garonne Apartments, located at 2663 Gilbert Avenue, to the Navarre Realty Company.[77]

5-29. The Garonne, 2663 Gilbert Avenue, ca. 1917 [78]

St. Francis De Sales Church at the corner of *Woodburn and Madison Roads* was designed by architect Francis G. Himpler in 1878 in the Gothic Revival style.[79] The Steinkamp brothers designed an addition to the *parish house* in 1919.[80]

In 1919, the brothers designed an "Agency House" for the *Cunningham-Holmes Company*, distributors of Pierce-Arrow cars and trucks on *Gilbert Avenue*. The building was two stories and contained 11,000 square feet.[81] This is now the location of a raised freeway ramp.

5-30. 1920 Pierce-Arrow [82]

In 1921, Joseph and Bernard designed a garage and service station for *Victor Strange* of the *Chevrolet Motor Car Company* on *Gilbert Avenue across from Florence Street* to cost $40,000. They were also taking bids for an adjoining building.[83–85] The building next to that was the office of a contemporary of the brothers, Cincinnati architect Harry Hake.[86]

5-31. Chevrolet Motor Car Company, 2350 Gilbert Avenue, ca. 1921

The following year, they designed an auto sales and service building for the *Mason Towle Company Dodge* auto agency on the corner of *Gilbert Avenue and Sinton Avenue* for $100,000.[87–89] The architecture was described at that time as an early Tudor type. Joseph's home in Price Hill, which he designed a few years later, contained some of the same elements of style as this building. In 2020 the building was the home of Planet Dance.

5-32. Mason Towle Company Dodge auto agency, 2230 Gilbert Avenue, ca. 1923 [89]

5-33. Planet Dance, ca. 2019

Mr. J. H. Reeve commissioned the brothers to design a two and one-half story duplex at *2223 Fulton Avenue* in 1922.[90] This building is no longer standing.

The *Cooper Building* on *Park Avenue* was built in 1928 by *Myers Y. Cooper* before he became Governor of Ohio in 1929. He built many interesting homes in the Walnut Hills and Hyde Park areas, and his construction company is still in existence today. The original design had 41 individual residences.[91] When the structure was built, electric elevators and underground parking were considered high tech, and only the most elite families could afford such luxuries.[92] Although the Steinkamps are listed as the architects for The Cooper, this cannot be confirmed. However, they are credited with designing an apartment building for Myers' brother, Sanson M. Cooper, in Avondale.

5-34. The Cooper Apartments, 2324 Park Avenue, ca. 1929 [91]

CHAPTER 6

Clifton, Corryville, and Mt. Auburn

The earliest known work of J. B. (Johann) Steinkamp on record was for the first building constructed on the *University of Cincinnati* campus in 1875. He was paid $650 ($14,000 in today's dollars) "for superintendence of University building."[1] Samuel Hannaford was the architect for the *University Building* on *Clifton Avenue*[2], which served as the original College of Medicine and was in use until 1895, when the university moved up the hill. The school used the building for several functions until it was demolished in 1935. Interestingly, the chief engineer for the Golden Gate Bridge, Joseph Strauss—who was a University of Cincinnati alumnus—incorporated several bricks from the University Building into one of the pylons of the bridge.[3]

6-1. University of Cincinnati, ca. 1875 [4]

What appears to be one of the first houses that Joseph Steinkamp designed in the Clifton area was a three-story home at *519 Liberty Street* on Liberty Hill in Mt. Auburn. This house, built in the Queen Anne style, was designed for Cincinnati lawyer *J.B. Krushing* in 1887. It later became known as the *John and Katherine Kohl House* and

6-2. 519 Liberty Street, John and Katherine Kohl House, ca. 1887

6-3. 3202 Glendora Street, ca. 1892 [11]

was the home of Graeter's Inc. CEO Richard Graeter.[5] It was featured in the *Cincinnati Magazine* in May of 2006[5] and again in September of 2016, when it was on the market for just over a half-million dollars.[6] It was also featured in the 1994 movie *Milk Money*[5] and was featured on a WCPO House Tour in 2016.[7] Although Joseph was working with his father at the time, only Joseph's name appears on the blueprints that have survived all these years.[7] This is noteworthy because Joseph was only nineteen years old at the time.[9]

Working in Corryville for the first time, Joseph designed a home for **Mr. Fred Kurz** (he was listed as Kurtz) at ***3202 Glendora Street*** in 1892 that cost $3,000.[10]

Joseph Steinkamp designed a two-story brick ***stable*** on ***McMillan Street*** for **William Kalling** in 1896.[12]

In 1896, ***Thomas Emery's Sons*** moved into Clifton, purchasing land to build the **Parkside Apartments** (3315–3317 Jefferson Avenue). Joseph and Bernard designed the Parkside Flats in Clifton for the Emerys in 1897.[13] Since Joseph had just taken his younger brother, Bernard, as a partner, the Parkside may have been one of their first collaborations on an apartment. Like Avondale, Clifton was a pastoral compound settled by Cincinnati's merchant class and annexed by the city in 1896. Streetcars had begun running on Ludlow Avenue in the late 1880s. The Parkside was the first large-scale apartment building built in Clifton and was an unusual shingle-style design, with 23 units arranged in a unique Y-shaped plan. This ingenious configuration enhanced privacy and maximized views of Burnet Woods, the adjoining park. The wooden shingle style was unusual for Cincinnati during this period, because most apartment buildings of this period were brick. In 2006, the Parkside was converted to condominiums with 27 units[14] and in 2008 it was placed on the National Register of Historic Places.[15]

6-4. The Parkside, 3315–3317 Jefferson Avenue, ca. 1897 [14]

"No coal will be used in these new flat buildings" read the headline in the *Cincinnati Enquirer* in 1897.[16] The article went on to say that "architect Steinkamp" completed plans for a magnificent block of four modern flat buildings of four stories. However, an article in the *Cincinnati Post* reported that it would only be two four-story buildings.[17] They were being built by the *Pitton Brothers*, "the well-known dye men," on *McMillan Street between Ohio and Clifton Avenues*. The buildings contained 66 rooms and cost a total of $30,000. Each flat was equipped with a gas range for cooking, and the buildings would be heated with hot water pipes.

The *Melbourne Flats* at *39 W. McMillan Street* was designed in 1898 by Joseph and Bernard. It was an important example of Neo-Classical architecture "…combining motifs from several popular classical styles from the turn-of-the-century."[18] It was originally built as a residence for young professionals, including physicians.[19] It was listed in the National Register of Historic Places in 1984.[20]

6-5. Melbourne Flats, 39 W. McMillan Street, ca. 1989

6-6. Melbourne Flats Stained-glass window [21]

Around 1900, the brothers designed the *Abbotsford Apartments* at *132–140 W. McMillan*.[22] The building was sold in 1957 and sometime after that was demolished for new construction on W. McMillan.[23]

6-7. The Abbotsford Apartments, ca. 1900 [22]

6-8. Hulbert Taft House, 439 Lafayette Avenue, ca. 1904 [26]

This elegant house, belonging to *Hulbert Taft Sr.*, nephew of President William Howard Taft, is on *Lafayette Avenue* in Clifton and was reported to have been designed by Joseph and Bernard in 1904.[24] The house, which is an example of Georgian Revival style, was enlarged to its present size in 1917 and was said to be a gift from Hulbert to his daughter, Katherine Taft Benedict, wife of James B. Benedict.[25]

The Kinsey is located at *2145 Maplewood Avenue* just outside the historic district of Mount Auburn, at the corner of Maplewood Avenue and Kinsey Avenue, with the primary facade facing Maplewood Avenue. It was commissioned by *C. W. Cole,* whose family planned to occupy the 10 rooms on the second floor. The three-story building is Beaux Arts in style and was constructed in 1906 at a cost of $30,000.[27, 28] This design is characteristic of a landmark building and is a good example of turn-of-the-century luxury apartment living in Cincinnati's first suburb. The exterior is a combination of stone and painted brick. The building recently underwent a considerable restoration. It was placed on the National Register of Historic Places in 2013.[29]

6-9. Kinsey Flats, 2415 Maplewood Avenue, ca. 1906 [29]

Thomas Emery's Sons named Joseph G. Steinkamp and Brothers *[sic]* to design a three-story brick and stone flat building on the south side of Ludlow Avenue, between Clifton and Whitfield Streets, in 1899. It was to cost $25,000.[30] This was most likely *The Roanoke*. Between 1900 and 1906, Joseph and Bernard designed five large apartment buildings in the Clifton area within about a two-block area. These included *The Roanoke* (ca. 1900) on Ludlow Avenue; *The Roslyn* (ca. 1904) and *The Romaine* (ca. 1905), both on Middleton Avenue; the *Maplewood* apartments (ca. 1905) on Telford Avenue; and *The Rutland* (ca. 1906) on Shiloh Avenue.

An article in the *Cincinnati Post* in 1904 proclaimed, "Bright building trade prospects indicated by architects' plans."[31] It described a "thoroughly modern" four-story structure, with separate servants' rooms for each flat, on the corner of Middleton and Shillito *[sic]* Avenues. The sketch of the flat building matches the final design of *The Rutland*, which is at Middleton and Shiloh Avenues. This $50,000 building added to the already long list of large apartments designed by the Steinkamp brothers and being built by Thomas Emery Sons. The cost of The Romaine was reported to be $23,000[32], while the cost of the Maplewood was put at $50,000.[33]

6-10. The Roanoke, 359 Ludlow Avenue, ca. 1900

6-11. The Roslyn, 3404–3420 Middleton Avenue, ca. 1904

6-12. The Romaine, 3421 Middleton Avenue, ca. 1905

6-13. Maplewood Apartments, 3440 Telford Street, ca. 1905 [29]

6-14. The Rutland, 358 Shiloh Street, ca. 1906

The brothers designed a modest wood and frame building for *Anthony Siegman* on *Rohs Street* in Clifton in 1904 at a cost of $2,500.[34]

6-15. 2368 Rohs Street, ca. 1904 [35]

A "St. Louis Flat" building at the corner of *Jefferson Avenue and Charlton Street* was designed by the Steinkamps for *Joseph Berning* in 1905.[36] It is quite possible that Joseph Steinkamp and Joseph Berning were acquainted as both were longtime members of the St. Aloysius Orphan Society.[37]

It was also reported the same year that they designed a three-story flat for *Mr. Berning* at the corner of *Jefferson Avenue and Rochelle Street* at a cost of $15,000.[38] This building was known at the *Josemil Flats*.[39] The building was sold in 1945 and was demolished sometime later to make way for the expansion of the University of Cincinnati.

6-16. 2704 Jefferson Avenue, ca. 1905

6-17. Josemil Flats, ca. 1905 [40]

In 1906, the brothers were designing a two-story "dry house," where spent grain is converted into animal feed, for the *Clifton Springs Distilling Company* on *Ludlow Avenue near Mill Creek*.[41] Later that year, it was reported that they were designing another building for the distillery, this one at one and one-half stories.[42]

6-18. Clifton Springs Distilling Company, ca. 1914 [43]

A couple of years later, the brothers designed an apartment building at the corner of *Brooklyne [sic] and Ludlow Avenues* for *Fred Holz* at a cost of $35,000.[44] It appears that this building is *The Brookline Apartments* that are still in use today.

6-19. The Brookline Apartments, 3401 Brookline Avenue, ca. 1907

Over a two-year span, the brothers designed three homes in Clifton. One was a two and one-half story home at *3321 Morrison Avenue* for *Walter Doerr*, built in 1907 at a cost of $7,000.[45, 46] Another was a two and one-half story home at 3439 *Middleton Avenue* near *Bryant Avenue* for *Charles E. Pierle*, owner of Wielert's Café on Vine Street.[46–48]

6-20. Doerr House at 3321 Morrison Avenue, ca. 1907

6-21. Charles Pierle house at 3439 Middleton Avenue, ca. 1905

One year later, they designed another two and one-half story home at the corner of *Middleton Avenue and Wood Avenue* for *William D. Baas* of the Baas Brothers Saloon and Cooperage.[49, 50]

6-22. Baas house at 3645 Middleton Avenue, ca. 1908

In 1908, the brothers designed a two-story flat building in Corryville at *310 Goodman Street* for *Mr. Peter Pickel*, owner of Peter and Co, Stonemasons, that cost $6,000.[51–53] It is now the site of University Hospital.

Shortly afterward, the brothers designed a three-story store and six, four-room apartments at the corner of *Vine and Nixon Streets* in Corryville for *William Peters*. The cost was put at $25,000, and the structure is now the *Mayflower Apartments*.[54, 55]

6-23. The Mayflower, 3201 Vine Street, ca. 1909

It was reported in the *Cincinnati Enquirer* in 1909 that the Steinkamps were designing a four-story house for **Mr. Richard Crane** on **Mulberry Street, east of Main Street** in Mt. Auburn.[56] This area is currently undergoing redevelopment and the house is no longer standing.

The brothers also drew up plans for a three-story apartment building on **Calhoun Avenue** for **Mr. Robert Laidlaw** of Sinton Avenue in 1910 at a cost of $15,000.[57, 58] What was most likely the same building was reported to be a 24-room apartment for Mrs. B. Laidlaw on Calhoun.[59]

Later, in 1914, the brothers designed a four-story building at the corner of **Vine and Charlton Streets** in Corryville for the **Finn estate** at a cost of $23,000.[60, 61] The location was formerly the site of an old blacksmith shop, which was torn down to make way for the new storehouse and flats.

6-24. Vine and Charlton, ca. 1914

The *Seton Realty Company* applied for a permit to erect a three-story brick apartment building designed by the Steinkamps on the corner of *Clifton Avenue and Gerard Street* in 1918 that would cost $40,000.[62, 63] However, no Cincinnati maps show these two streets crossing at any time, and the location of the apartment building remains a mystery.

CHAPTER 7

Price Hill, Delhi, Westwood, and South Fairmont

It appears that Joseph and Bernard first became involved with construction on the west side of Cincinnati just after the turn of the century, shortly after Joseph moved his family to Suire Avenue in 1902. Early on, it must have been quite a commute for young Joseph. Did he take the Price Hill Incline to get to his office? Joseph continued to live and work in the area until his death in 1948. Together, the brothers designed homes, apartments, churches, schools, and a splendid Art Deco waterworks on the west side of Cincinnati.

In June of 1902, Joseph G. Steinkamp purchased two lots from Hannah A. Suire in the Samuel A. Suire subdivision in Price Hill, for the price of $3,850.[1] The house at *912 Suire Avenue* that became the Steinkamp family home was built ca. 1869, but Joseph is credited with designing the addition on its south side. The addition contains a storage compartment under a window seat that is a perfect size for holding house plans. Is it possible that Joseph used the addition as an office? Joseph and Laura lived here with their sons, Albert and Eugene, until he built a house next door at 916 Suire Avenue in 1928.[2] Following the sale of that home at auction in 1929, the family moved back into the house at 912 Suire, where they lived until moving to Anderson Ferry Road in 1934.

7-1. Joseph's home at 912 Suire Avenue, ca. 1869

Starting around 1904, the Steinkamp brothers started what was a flurry of activity in Price Hill, designing more than a dozen homes over the next five years. That year, they designed a home for *William A. Kaiser* at *1234 Ross Avenue* at a cost of $2,000, the first of many two and one-half story homes in the area. At the time, Mr. Kaiser lived across the street at 1239 Ross.[3]

Their next known work on the west side was designing a double two and one-half story home for *Mrs. Minnie Hazard*, an intermediate schoolteacher, on *W. Eighth Street* in 1904.[4]

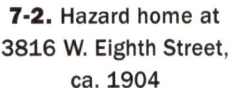
7-2. Hazard home at 3816 W. Eighth Street, ca. 1904

The following year, the brothers designed a three-story apartment for *Mrs. D. W. Bellville* on the corner of *W. Eighth Street and Purcell Avenue* in Price Hill. It was estimated to cost $20,000.[5] This building was restored to its former beauty by the Price Hill Will nonprofit organization in 2016.[6]

7-3. Apartment at 751–757 Purcell Avenue, ca. 1905

The Elberon (Robertson) Apartments

The brothers designed the *Robinson [sic] Apartments* (later to be known as the *Elberon*) at the corner of *Elberon Avenue and W. Eighth Street,* reportedly in 1905, for *Roberson [sic] Realty* at a cost of $100,000.[9] However, another source lists the cost at $125,000 and reported it had 77 rooms divided into 17 suites.[10] Five years later, Musco M. Robertson, President of the Robertson Reality Company[a], sold the building to W. F. Robertson for $120,000.[11] That same year, the brothers designed a building at 7th and Race streets downtown for M. M. Robertson.[12]

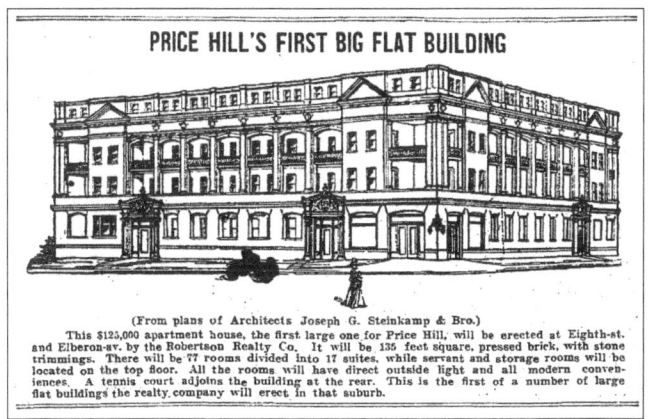

7-4. Early sketch of Robertson Apartments, 3414 W. Eighth Street, ca. 1905 [7]

7-5. The Elberon (Robertson) Apartments, ca. 1905 [8]

In 1929, an advertisement for the Elberon in the *Cincinnati Enquirer* listed "a beautiful 5-room apartment and maid's room complete with heat and janitor service, storage, and garage (if desired)." The advertisement also noted that the apartment building was a stop on the streetcar line.[13] Over the years, the once beautiful building fell into neglect and became an eyesore on its corner lot in Price Hill. Finally, ground was broken in February of 2011 for the start of renovations, after the building had been abandoned for over a decade. Hundreds of people attended a celebration on April 12, 2012, for the opening of the renovated building. Price Hill Will, the Model Group, the City of Cincinnati, and several other development agencies worked together on the

---

[a] Robertson Reality Company is the correct spelling of the name of the company.

7-6. Elberon Apartments, ca. 2016

$7.4 million renovation. The Elberon now features 37 affordable apartments for senior citizens 55 years and older.[14]

Another of their early homes in Price Hill was a two and one-half story flat building for *Alice and Mary Paddack* on the west side of *Vaughn Avenue* (later Fifth Avenue and now *Rosemont Avenue*).[15] Alice was a librarian and Mary a schoolteacher.[16]

7-7. 525 Rosemont Avenue, ca. 1906 [17]

In 1906, the brothers designed two homes for *Henry F. Lackman* in Price Hill.[18] Mr. Lackman lived on Rapid Run Pike in the mansion that was later purchased by the bootlegger George Remus.[19] At that time, Henry was president of the Herman Lackman Brewing Company.[20] The location of the two homes was not reported. However, Henry Lackman owned property at the corner of W. Eighth Street and Hermosa Avenue in 1910, and in 1920 he was living at 4373 Carnation Avenue, so these may have been the locations of the two homes.[21, 22]

Still in 1906, the brothers designed a seven-room bungalow for *Joseph Kealy* on *Hawthorne Avenue*.[23] In 1912 Joseph lived at 500 Hawthorne Street, but the house is no longer there.[24]

Also, the same year, they designed a one and one-half story brick home on the west side of *Purcell Avenue* for *John B. Osthoff* at a cost of $2,700.[25]

7-8. Osthoff home at 459 Purcell Avenue, ca. 1906

After Joseph moved to *Suire Avenue*, he and Bernard designed several homes on the street in addition to the immediate area. In 1906, they designed a two and one-half story home for *Anna G. Vonderahe* at a cost of $4,000.[26]

7-9. Vonderahe home at 816 Suire Avenue, ca. 1906

It was reported in 1907 that the brothers designed an apartment on *Eighth Street* across from Suire Avenue for *Louis Menke* at a cost of $5,000 or $6,000.[27, 28] It was later reported that Mrs. E. Menke was building a two-story flat on the south side of W. Eighth Street at a cost of $6,000.[29] Laura Steinkamp's mother, Elizabeth, lived at this address.[30, 31] Louis was the brother of Elizabeth's late husband, John. Both Louis and John were former Cincinnati policemen.[32]

7-10. Menke apartment at 3961 W. Eighth Street, ca. 1907 [33]

That same year, the Steinkamp brothers were making plans for a "*St. Louis Flat*" on the west side of *Suire Avenue*.[34] It was to be an eight-room flat and across Suire Avenue from the Steinkamp home at 912 Suire to cost $6,000. This was another apartment built for *Louis Menke*.

7-11. Menke home at 905 Suire Avenue, ca. 1907

The following year the brothers designed one more home on Suire Avenue. It was also two and one-half stories and was built for ***Mr. A. M. Braun*** at ***833 Suire***.[35] Mr. Andrew M. Braun was one of Father Roth's lay advisors for the new church construction project.[36]

7-12. Braun home at 833 Suire Avenue, ca. 1908

Nearby, on *Sunset Avenue,* the brothers designed a one-story brick home for *H. H. Zugelter* at a cost of $3,000 in 1907.³⁷ However, Mr. Herman H. Zugelter was listed in 1908 at 945 Sunset Avenue, which is a two-story home.³⁸ The home at 945 Sunset was built in 1906, so it is possible a two-story structure was built instead of a one-story.³⁹

7-13. Zugelter home at 945 Sunset Avenue, ca. 1907

Also, in 1907, the brothers designed a two-story apartment building on *Eighth and Evans streets* for *Mrs. E. Montifer* that contained four apartments.[40] This area is now the site of the Eighth Street viaduct, and the building is no longer standing. The same year, it was also reported that the Steinkamps were designing a similar flat building on Eighth Street across from Suire Avenue to cost $6,000.[41] This was probably an error because the only listing in *Williams' Cincinnati Directory* (1910) for Montifer was at 1901 Eighth Street near Evans.[42]

The Ohio Architect and Builder reported in 1908 that the brothers drew up plans for two brick homes of seven rooms each on *Oakland Avenue* in Price Hill for *Mr. John Oberhelman*, president and owner of the J.A. Oberhelman Foundry Company.[43] Mr. Oberhelman lived nearby at Olive and St. Lawrence Streets.[44]

Again in Price Hill, the brothers designed a home to be built on *Murdock Avenue* in 1908 for *E. H. Hartman* at a cost of $4,000.[45] In 1910 Mr. Ernest H. Hartman lived at 408 Considine Avenue on the corner of Murdock Avenue, but that home is listed as being built in 1891.[46]

Continuing with their flurry of activity in Price Hill, the Steinkamp brothers designed yet another two and one-half story home on *Fisher (now Pedretti) Avenue* for *Mr. Joseph C. Stein*, superintendent of bridges, at a cost of $2,500.[47, 48]

7-14. Stein home at 810 Pedretti Avenue, ca. 1909 [49]

The brothers designed a two and one-half story home on *Homestead Place* in Westwood for a *Mr. Henry Vonderhaar* of Western Avenue (now Beekman) in 1910 at a cost of $6,000 to $7,500.[50, 51]

7-15. Vonderhaar home at 2504 Homestead Place, ca. 1910

The same year, they designed another two and one-half story home at *915 Suire Avenue* directly across from Joseph's home. It was built for *Catherine Crone* of Summit Avenue at a cost of $4,000.[52]

7-16. Crone home at 915 Suire Avenue, ca. 1910

Another was for *Mrs. Catherine Forn* in 1910 on Suire Avenue, but the address was not given.[53] However, in 1928 Katherine Forn lived at 839 Suire Avenue, that was built in 1923.[54]

Still in 1910, the brothers designed another home in Price Hill on *Elberon Avenue* for *John Forbeck* at a cost of $5,500.⁵⁵ It cannot be confirmed that this home was ever built, as John's widow was listed at a different address in 1912.⁵⁶

In 1913, Joseph and Bernard designed a home on *Academy Avenue* in Price Hill and a store with apartments on *Warsaw Avenue*. The home at *861 Academy Avenue* was for *George H. Feltes*, Secretary and Treasurer for the *U.S. Electric Tool Company* on W. Eighth Street. It was a two and one-half story stucco house.⁵⁷, ⁵⁸ Five years later, they designed a new factory for the company on W. Sixth Street.⁵⁹

7-17. Feltes home at 861 Academy Avenue, ca. 1913

The Warsaw Avenue store, with apartments above and an attached bake shop, was a two-story brick building with limestone trim and cost $10,000. *Julius Hellenschmidt*, who lived on Warsaw Avenue, was the owner.⁶⁰⁻⁶² This is the same building at *3640 Warsaw Avenue* that the brothers renovated for the *Provident Savings Bank and Trust Company* in 1919 and that eventually became the headquarters for the *Price Hill Historical Society* (see below).

St. William Parish Churches and School

In their first of several collaborations with Reverend Francis Roth and *St. William Roman Catholic Church*, in 1910 the Steinkamps designed a *temporary church building* to seat 400 people. It was located on *Fifth Avenue* (now *Rosemont Avenue*) on the corner of *Reed Avenue* (now *St. William Avenue*) in 1910. The temporary church was built the following year on a piece of property owned by Mr. Herman Elsaesser.⁶³, ⁶⁴

The St. William's Men's Society was organized in 1910 and Joseph Steinkamp was elected Vice President of the group. Also organized that year was the St. Ann Society, of which Laura Steinkamp was elected as its first President. It was also reported that Joseph was one of three contributors who donated the bells of the first St. William church.⁶⁴

7-18. St. William Roman Catholic Church, Fifth Avenue, ca. 1911 [65]

In 1911, the Steinkamps were commissioned to draw up plans for a new school building for *St. William Parish*, on the corner of *Sunset Avenue and W. Eighth Street*, that was estimated to cost $38,500. Archbishop Moeller officiated at the school's dedication in Price Hill in August of 1912, following a 1,000-person parade from the Incline to the school.[64, 65] In 1915 they designed a two-room $10,000 addition to the school building because of the growing enrollment.[66] The 1911 church was moved down St. William Street next to the school around 1915 and was used as part of the school until it was demolished in 1954.[64, 67]

7-19. St. William School, 4125 St. Williams Avenue, ca. 1912 [64]

7-20. St. William School, ca. 2021

The Steinkamps' work for St. William Parish continued in 1922 with the addition of the Parish House, costing about $25,000.⁶⁸

7-21. St. William Parish House, ca. 1922

In 1929, the Steinkamps designed a spectacular new church to replace the old *St. William Church*, under the guidance of ***Rev. Francis A. Roth***. The cost of this beautiful structure in the Romanesque Revival style was $400,000 (about $6 million in 2020 currency). The church was part of a half-million-dollar parish development program that included the rectory and sisters' house.⁶⁹ St. William Church was named after

St. William the Abbot and Archbishop William Elder, and Archbishop John T. McNicholas presided over the dedication on October 4, 1931.[70] Among the church's many beautiful features are the 12 Italian marble columns, one for each apostle. The 18-foot great rose stained-glass window was created by the G. C. Riordan Studio in 1940. In order to pay off the massive debt incurred in the church's construction, Reverend Francis Reardon started what is believed to be the first bingo games sponsored by a church.[64]

7-22. St. William Church, 4108 W. Eighth Street, ca. 1931 [69]

7-23. St. William Church [71]

The brothers are credited with designing a home for *W. W. Oskamp* on *Harrison Avenue* in 1909. However, the house is also attributed to another Cincinnati architect, W.W. Franklin.[72] Since both firms had other connections to the Oskamp family, it is difficult to determine who actually designed this home.

7-24. Oskamp home at 2440 Harrison Avenue, ca. 1909 [73]

Dr. Louis E. Cook had a small, two-story office designed by the Steinkamps at *3582 Warsaw Avenue* in 1915 for $3,000.[74] However, Dr. Cook's office is listed as being at 3532 in 1916 and for several years after that.[75] Sometime later, Dr. Cook moved to 3652 Warsaw Avenue.[76]

7-25. Office of Dr. Louis E. Cook at 3532 Warsaw Avenue, ca. 1915 [77]

The brothers were reportedly designing a two-story residence in 1917 at *822 Rosemont Avenue* in Price Hill for *Joseph Middendorf* that cost $5,000.[78] However, there was never a house at 822 Rosemont Avenue, and no one named Middendorf (or similar names) ever lived on Rosemont Avenue.

In 1918, the brothers designed a two-story factory for the *U.S. Electric Tool Company* valued at $15,000. This was located at *Sixth Street and Mt. Hope* in East Price Hill.[79] In 1913, they had designed a home in Price Hill for *George H. Feltes*, then Secretary and Treasurer of the tool company.

7-26. U.S. Electric Tool Company, 2490 River Road, ca. 1918

The Steinkamp brothers were the architects for the auditorium/clubhouse for the *Price Hill Knights of Columbus* on *Warsaw Avenue* near *Garfield Avenue* (now Fairbanks Avenue) in 1919 at a cost of $22,000.[80, 81]

7-27. Knights of Columbus Clubhouse, Fairbanks Avenue, ca. 1919 [82]

Also, in 1919, the brothers designed a $1,500 one-story addition to a home at *1021 Del Monte Place* in Price Hill for *Charles Schell* and converted a residence to two apartments at *715 Purcell Avenue* for *Charles F. Taylor* for $2,300.[83]

The Steinkamp brothers were commissioned to make plans for the necessary changes to the existing storeroom at *3640 Warsaw Avenue* for the new quarters for the Price Hill

Branch of the *Provident Savings Bank and Trust Company*.[84] This is the same building they designed a few years earlier for *Julius Hellenschmidt*. In 2000, the building became the headquarters and museum for the *Price Hill Historical Society*.[85]

7-28. Price Hill Historical Society Museum, 3640 Warsaw Avenue, ca. 1913

Joseph and Laura's Home on Suire Avenue

In April 1927, Joseph Steinkamp purchased two lots on the east side of Suire Avenue in Price Hill from Marion L. Suire for one dollar each.[86] The following year Joseph completed his new home and moved from his house at *912 Suire Avenue* to the new house next door at *916 Suire Avenue*. This house has been called "The Little Stone House," owing to its small stature when viewed from the street. However, with a walk-out basement, it is a full three stories in the back.

This house contains considerable detail and is probably one of Joseph's most meticulous building designs. It appears that he may have designed his home to showcase his talents as an architect. Owing to its unique details and construction, the house has been featured in the *Cincinnati Enquirer* and the *Price Hill Press*.[87–89]

7-29. Joseph and Laura's home at 916 Suire Avenue, ca. 1928 [87]

Both the living room and the dining room feature cathedral ceilings with hand-stenciled beams, intricately designed terrazzo floors, and large wrought iron chandeliers adorned with brass figures. Similar brass figures perform a German folk dance on wrought iron sconces that circle the living room. The limestone fireplace, tucked in a corner of the living room, is decorated with carved figures and a quote from Longfellow's

7-30. 916 Suire Avenue [88]

The Builders. On one wall of the dining room, carved Beefeaters are ready to serve a meal to guests seated at the dining room table, which overlooks a small balcony. The exterior of the home is a mix of wood, stucco, stone, and "clinker or klinker bricks"[b] blended into a unique mosaic. The front of the house is unique, with the Steinkamp coat of arms in stained glass high above the living room and three "envy heads" carved at the peak of the master bedroom. Distinctive features of the bathroom are Rookwood tiles and a walk-in shower with a "needle" shower.

7-31, 7-32, 7-33. Envy heads

In 1927, Joseph had put the house at 912 Suire up for sale.[90] An advertisement in the *Cincinnati Enquirer* in April 1928[92] states that it is for sale "…at a remarkably low price for a quick sale, as my new home is now ready for occupancy." The following month[93], the new ad said it "must be sold this month." However, a few days later another ad appeared in the *Enquirer* for his new home at 916 Suire, stating "New residence of distinctive design and construction: stone, brick and timber…" and ending with "offer wanted." [94] Next, in July, yet more ads appeared offering "New English stone, brick and timber house…any reasonable offer considered.[95, 96] One final ad appeared, offering the house for $23,000.[97] Interestingly, a couple of weeks earlier, Mrs. Steinkamp entertained 50 guests in her "beautiful new home" with dinner and bridge, where "Mrs. Anna Steinkamp won first

---

[b] A clinker brick or klinker brick is one that was discarded because it was discolored or distorted. In the 1920s, leaders of the Arts and Crafts design movement rediscovered their possibilities for creative and dramatic architectural detailing.

7-34. 916 Suire Avenue

prize and Mrs. Benjamin *[sic]* Steinkamp won the consolation prize."[98] Joseph once again tried to sell the house at 912 Suire in early 1929 for a price of $16,000.[99]

7-35. Steinkamp coat of arms

7-36. Ad for auction of Joseph's and Laura's home, 1929 [100]

Unfortunately, the Steinkamp's new home went up for public auction on September 1 of that year[100] and sold for $16,500 to Mr. Clifford B. Sieve[101], and Joseph and his family moved back to 912 Suire. It is puzzling that Joseph tried to sell his new home shortly after he moved in. Had he gone into debt with all the fine features that he included in his new home? Since he still owned the house at 912 Suire, why didn't he put that up for auction instead of his new home? Indeed, it must have been a sad day for the Steinkamp family when they moved their belongings back into their previous home and then watched as a new family moved into their beautiful home.

Around 1934 the Steinkamps moved to the Delhi neighborhood, and in 1936 the home at 912 Suire sold at auction.[102]

7-37, 7-38, 7-39, 7-40, 7-41, 7-42. Etched figures on windows

In 1920, Joseph and Bernard drew up plans for a bungalow-type house at *5721 Glenway Avenue* for *Edward A. Schwartz*.[103, 104] However, Mr. Schwartz's address was listed as *4519 Glenway Avenue* in 1922.[105] A bungalow style house stood at number 4519 in 1922, so that may be the one designed by the brothers.

7-43. Schwartz home at 4519 Glenway Avenue, ca. 1921 [106]

In the midst of the Depression, the brothers, along with Gillespie and Felsberg, designed a unique tiny house of about 600 sq. ft. for *Mrs. Florence Lester* that would cost only $2,500.[107] The design was for four or five rooms, but it could be laid out in ten different floor plans. It was located at *4534 Lower River Road* and was demolished ca. 1985.

The concept of a relatively inexpensive home during the years of the Depression probably was quite appealing. Was this why Joseph and Bernard lent their names to this project or was it a possible way to bring in a little extra money during this time—or maybe both? Interestingly, a few years later in April 1936, *Architectural Forum* devoted an entire issue to "The Five Thousand Dollar House."[108]

The brothers are credited with designing a home on *Vittmer Avenue* in Westwood about 1933 for *J. H. Dickman*. The article in the *Enquirer* stated that Peter Meyer bought the home in 1934 and that it was located at *3542 Vittmer Avenue*.[c, 109, 110] However, in 1935, Richard Meyer lived at *3265 Vittmer* in a home built in 1933 that is identical to the sketch of the home but is a mirror-image of the sketch.[111]

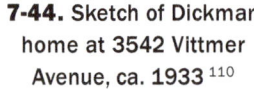

7-44. Sketch of Dickman home at 3542 Vittmer Avenue, ca. 1933 [110]

7-45. 3265 Vittmer, ca. 1933 [112]

The same year, Joseph and his associates were involved with designing an *"American Beauty Home"* in Westwood on *Ferguson Road* near Queen City Avenue.[113] Shortly afterwards, an ad appeared in the *Cincinnati Enquirer* for such a home that had been designed by "one of Cincinnati's leading architects," presumable the Steinkamps.[114]

---

[c] Street numbers on Vittmer Avenue do not go above 3300.

7-46. American Beauty Home, 3029 Veazey Avenue, ca. 1933 [115]

◀ **7-47.** Ad for American Beauty Homes [113]

In 1934, Joseph designed a 5-room home at *1022 Anderson Ferry Road* and lived there until he moved in with Albert around 1944. The house had a lap pool and two fishponds.[116] In 1937, he designed a much larger house across the street at number *1011* for his sister-in-law, *Martha Menke Siefke,* and her husband Ed. Gillespie and Felsberg collaborated on the design of this house. Both houses had distinctive weathervanes. The weathervane on the house at 1022 had three cats and the one at 1011 had Mother Goose, which survives today.[117]

7-48. Joseph and Laura's home at 1022 Anderson Ferry Road, ca. 1934 [118]

7-49. Siefke home at 1011 Anderson Ferry Road, ca. 1937

The brothers and their two partners, Gillespie and Felsberg, designed a home for *Ray Treinen* on *Cleves-Warsaw Pike* in Price Hill in 1936. The home included "… three baths, a rathskeller, complete insulation, and gas-fired air-conditioning…" with a built-in double garage.[119] Interestingly, the home was built as a mirror-image of the original sketch, similar to the home on Vittmer.

7-50. Treinen home, ca. 1936 [119]

7-51. Treinen home at 5024 Cleves-Warsaw Pike, ca. 1936

In 1936, Joseph and Bernard, assisted by Gillespie and Felsberg, designed a two-apartment building on *Harrison Avenue* in Westwood for *Mrs. Emma Kerl and Mrs. Johanna Hellman*. The apartments had gas-fired air-conditioning; one unit had five rooms and the other had four.[120]

7-52. Kerl/Hellman duplex at 2934 Harrison Avenue, ca. 1936 [120]

7-53. Duplex on Harrison Avenue, ca. 2017

Western Hills Pumping Station

In 1936, Joseph and Bernard completed plans for the *Western Hills Pumping Station* for the *Waterworks Department*, to be built on *Queen City Avenue* in South Fairmont. The projected cost was $218,500, and it was to be built by the David Gordon Construction Company.[121] When it was completed in December 1937 at a cost of $312,000, it was called "the most modern in the United States." The new pumping station was powered entirely by electricity, as opposed to the old steam-powered pumping station that it replaced.[122]

The Art Deco building designed by the Steinkamp brothers was a monument to their desire to provide a structure that visitors would marvel at for years to come. The first thing one notices when approaching the one-story limestone building is the large fresco of a muscular figure pouring a vase of water above the

7-54. Western Hill Pumping Station, 1650 Queen City Avenue, ca. 1937[122]

7-55. Western Hills Pumping Station [125]

front door and surrounded by lightning bolts. To either side of the figure are metal-paneled Egyptian water carriers that cap off elongated glass block windows.[123] Next to the doors is a quote from Byron, "Till taught by pain—men really know not what good water's worth."[124]

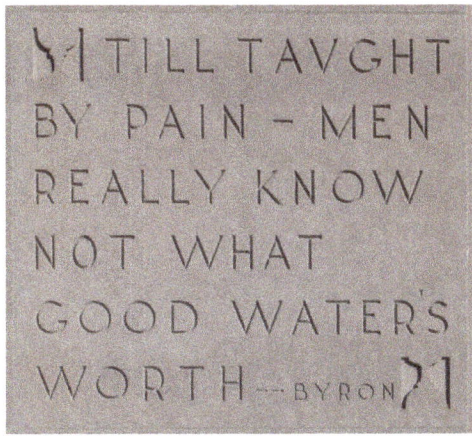

7-56. Byron quote on building [123]

7-57. Figure with lightning bolts [123]

Joseph Steinkamp and Felsberg & Gillespie were the architects for a two and one-half story addition to the *Westwood First Presbyterian Church* at *3011 Harrison Avenue*, built in 1936 at a cost of $65,000.[126]

7-58. Addition to Westwood First Presbyterian Church, 3011 Harrison Avenue, ca. 1936

Not far away from the church, Joseph and Bernard designed a home for *James Harwood Garrison* at the corner of *Urwiler and Hazelwood Avenues* in 1937. A medallion fashioned from a silver dollar on the newel post has the names of the architects engraved on it.[127] James was the father of Cincinnati comedian Harry Garrison who started the Cincinnati Player Piano Company in 1957.[128]

7-59. Garrison home at 2855 Urwiler Avenue, ca. 1937

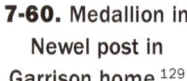

7-60. Medallion in Newel post in Garrison home [129]

Next door to the Garrison house, the four architects again teamed up to design another home, in April 1938, for *Henry Nagle* at the corner of *Montana and Hazelwood Avenues*. The three and one-half story, nine-room home featured a maid's room and a three-car garage and was built at a cost of $30,000.[130]

7-61. Nagle home at 3410 Hazelwood Avenue, ca. 1938

Joseph was involved with *Suire Avenue* one last time when he applied for a modification of the Building Zone Code for an addition to the home of *Mr. Adam Nicolai* at *824 Suire*.[131] Mr. Nicolai had been a lay advisor to Fr. Roth for the construction project for the new St. William Church.[64]

CHAPTER 8

St. Bernard

One might wonder why Joseph and Bernard Steinkamp would venture all the way to St. Bernard as early as the 1890s to design a home for the Nurre family. Travel for such a distance was not easy at that time. The Steinkamps and Nurre families may have known each other, as they emigrated from the same area of Germany and the Nurre picture frame and moldings shop on Plum Street was only two blocks from the Steinkamp offices on W. Court Street downtown. Surely, the brothers would have specified moldings in their building designs.

Joseph and Bernard Steinkamp first ventured into St. Bernard in 1892 when they designed a two and one-half story home for *Mr. H. Nurre* at a cost of $2,200.[1] This was the home of Henry and Mary Nurre at the corner of *Church and Burnet Streets*.

8-1. Nurre house at 171 Church Street, ca. 1892

In 1905 the brothers completed plans for *Henry Imwalle*, the Mayor-elect of St. Bernard, for a three-story building on the corner of *Carthage Pike* (now Vine Street) and *Starchtown Road* (now Bank Avenue). It was planned to contain two stores and seven flats.[2, 3]

8-2. Henry Imwalle Funeral Parlor, ca. 1912 [4]

The Steinkamps designed a three-story store and apartment for *Edward Grunkermeyer* in St. Bernard in 1906.[5] However, no details about the location were provided.

The brothers prepared plans in 1907 for the rebuild of a *"press house"* for the *Emery Candle Company*, located in Ivorydale, at a cost of $3,500.[6] A press house is where the blocks of candle stock are subjected to cold and extremely high pressures.[7]

Also, in 1907, the Steinkamps designed an addition to *St. Clement's School* on Vine Street that added three additional classrooms.[8, 9]

One of the brothers' more unusual designs was for a *tunnel* for the Cincinnati, Hamilton and Dayton Railroad at the *Emery Candle Works* in 1917, at a cost of $3,000.[10] It was eventually abandoned and sealed up.

8-3. Tunnel at Emery Candle Works, ca. 1917 [11]

In 1919, the *City of St. Bernard* issued a bond for $65,000 for an engine house and equipment.[12] Joseph and Bernard were receiving bids on the structure in 1920.[13] They designed a two-story *fire engine house* and equipment. It was on the corner of *Carthage Pike (Vine Street) and Clay Street*.[14] The previous firehouse had been in the rear of the old Town Hall. The building was demolished to make way for the construction of I-75.[15]

8-4. St. Bernard Fire House, ca. 1920 [4]

Also, in 1920, the brothers developed plans for interior renovations to the *St. Bernard Town (City) Hall*, to cost $20,000.[16] The firehouse can be seen at the far left, with the drying tower for the hoses, in the photo below.

8-5. St. Bernard Town Hall, ca. 1910

Still in 1920, the brothers drew plans for renovations to the *Imwalle Undertaker Company's* property, consisting of a new chapel and changes to the offices.[16]

The *Citizens' Bank of St. Bernard* purchased the three-story building in which the bank was located in 1920.[17] The following month, it was reported that Joseph and Bernard were designing a three-story bank building at the corner of *Carthage Pike and Bank Street* for Citizens' Bank of St. Bernard.[18]

8-6. Citizens' Bank of St. Bernard, ca. 1920 [4]

The following year, the brothers continued their work in St. Bernard, designing a funeral director's building plus apartments for *Frank Imwalle*, on *Carthage Avenue* (Vine Street). It was to be two and one-half stories and to contain apartments.[19] In May of the same year, the *Cincinnati Enquirer* reported that the Steinkamps were designing a new funeral parlor for *Henry Imwalle & Company* (The Imwalle Memorial) at 4811 Carthage Avenue.[20] In June of 2018, the George Wiedemann Brewing Company opened in the former Henry Imwalle funeral parlor.[21]

8-7. The Imwalle Memorial, 4811 Vine Street, ca. 1921 [22]

8-8. The Imwalle Memorial, 4811 Vine Street [4]

8-9. The George Wiedemann Brewing Company

Thirty years after they designed a house for the Nurre family, Joseph and Bernard drew up plans for a brick duplex for *Joseph Nurre* on *Errun Lane* in St. Bernard.[22] Interestingly, Errun is Nurre spelled backwards.

8-10. Nurre duplex, 4343 Errun Lane, ca. 1922

In what appears to be their last journey into St. Bernard, the brothers designed renovations and an addition to the home of *Frank A. Meyer* at *4253 Bertus Street* in 1923.[23] The home was originally built ca. 1866.[24]

8-11. Meyer home at 4253 Bertus Street, ca. 1866 [25]

CHAPTER 9

Hyde Park

Starting in 1912, Joseph and Bernard designed several homes in the Hyde Park area for prominent Cincinnati businessmen.

In 1912, it was reported that Benjamin *[sic]*[a] Steinkamp broke his arm in a fall while working on the home of ***Joseph (J.J.) Castellini*** on ***Edwards Road*** in Hyde Park.[1] However, records show that this home was built in 1906. The brothers may have been involved in renovations to the Castellini home, since they also worked on other buildings for Mr. Castellini around this time.

9-1. Castellini home at 1242 Edwards Avenue, ca. 1912

The following year, 1913, undertaker ***William G. Siefke*** purchased property at the corner of ***Michigan and Observatory Avenues*** in Hyde Park for construction of an eight-room brick house. Joseph G. Steinkamp and Bros. were responsible for designing the home.[2] The brothers also designed a home for William's son, Ed Siefke, Joseph's brother-in-law, in Delhi and a funeral parlor for the Siefke family.[3]

---

[a] Here and elsewhere, Bernard is sometimes incorrectly referred to as "Benjamin."

9-2. Siefke home at Observatory and Michigan Avenues, ca. 1913

In 1907, the brothers designed an apartment on *Maple Street* in Avondale for *C. E. Schaffner*, owner of the Cincinnati Garter Company.[4] Two years later, Mr. Schaffner bought a home on Stettinius Avenue in Hyde Park and probably built a new home on the site.[5] It is not known whether the Steinkamps were involved with its design. Early in 1914, Joseph and Bernard designed a *garage* for Mr. Schaffner for his home on Stettinius Avenue.[6]

In August, an article in the *Brick and Clay Record* stated that Joseph and Bernard were designing "…one of the handsomest and most unusual residences in the city, to be constructed for a well-known merchant." White enameled brick was to be used in its construction. The elegant home was on Observatory Avenue.[7] That year, the brothers designed a home on *Observatory Avenue* for Mr. Schaffner.[8] The plans for his home called for enameled brick so it is probably the home mentioned in the aforementioned article. Unfortunately, in 2010, this beautiful home was heavily damaged by fire, but it has recently undergone a restoration.[9]

The same year, the brothers were making plans for the *Georgian Terrace Flats* nearby, on *Madison Road*, for Mr. Schaffner.[10–12] The building was to have 12 four-room flats and cost $75,000. However, in October, the *Cincinnati Enquirer* reported that there had been a "slight glitch" in the plans: a small plot of adjoining property needed for the construction was no longer for sale, and the location would have to be moved closer to Madison Road.[13] In March 1916, it was listed again in *The American Contractor* as being on Madison Road and costing $50,000.[14] It was later described as "a stylish, three-story, 14-flat building highlighted by visually prominent 'East' and 'West' entrances…," completed at a cost of $75,000.[15] Whatever the final configuration and cost, it was and remains a very stylish building on Madison Road.

9-3. Home of C. E. Schaffner at 2460 Observatory Avenue, ca. 1914

9-4. Ad for Georgian Terrace Flats [16]

9-5. Georgian Terrace Flats at 2136 Madison Road, ca. 1914

The Steinkamp brothers were the architects for a house for *Mr. and Mrs. John H. Hall* at *3445 Observatory Place*, the cul-de-sac leading up to the Cincinnati Observatory in Hyde Park. In 1923, the *Cincinnati Enquirer* reported that Mrs. Hall had designed the residence and the brothers drew up the plans. It was to be built by the Leibold-Ferrell Building Company in the Tudor-Gothic architectural style of England at a price of $20,000. At the time, Mr. Hall managed the real estate department for Thomas Emery's Sons.[17, 18]

9-6. Hall home at 3445 Observatory Place, ca. 1923

The last evidence of the brothers' involvement with homes in Hyde Park is from 1938. They and their partners, Gillespie and Felsberg, designed a three-story home for *Charles E. Bishop* in February of that year at the corner of *Perkins Lane and Stettinius Avenue*.[19] This Hyde Park home featured a library and a built-in two-car garage.

9-7. Bishop home at Perkins Lane and Stettinius Avenue, ca. 1938 [19]

9-8. A current image, showing the Bishop home as virtually unchanged

CHAPTER 10

Evanston

Joseph and Bernard Steinkamp were active in Evanston, designing a magnificent church and school, a movie theater, and several commercial buildings, plus a home or two. Additionally, Bernard made his home on Clarion Avenue for most of his adult life.

In 1904, the Steinkamps started designing buildings for *A. L. Pachoud* of A. L. Pachoud & Co. The Pachouds were realtors and builders and had an office in the Mercantile Library Building, a few floors below the Steinkamps' offices.[1] The brothers would go on to design more buildings in Evanston and elsewhere for the firm.

That year, the brothers designed two homes on *Stacey Avenue* of nine rooms for *Mr. Pachoud*, each at a total cost of $5,000.[2]

Next, they designed six, two and one-half story brick and stone residences for *Mr. Pachoud* on *Wabash Avenue* between Clarion and Langdon Streets that cost $5,000 each.[3] These houses are still standing at 3612 to 3624 Wabash Avenue.[4]

In 1906, they designed a two and one-half story stone and brick dwelling on *Montgomery Road* between Jonathan and Sidney Avenues for *Mr. Pachoud* at a cost of $3,000.[5] Interstate I-71 now occupies this piece of property.

Almost next door on the corner of *Montgomery Road and Jonathan Avenue* is the *LaSalle Apartments* building designed by Joseph and Bernard Steinkamp for *Mr. Packard* also in 1906. It had 12 apartments and was described as "strictly modern and up-to-date."[6, 7]

10-1. LaSalle Apartments, 3501 Montgomery Road, ca. 1906

In 1906 *Bernard Steinkamp* purchased a lot at *1931 Clarion Avenue,* and his home was built in 1907.[8] One would assume that Bernard, probably with help from Joseph, designed the home. Bernard lived in this house with his wife, Clara, until his death in 1943.

10-2. Bernard and Clara's home at 1931 Clarion Avenue, ca. 1907

The brothers designed a *Sisters' Home* at *Montgomery Pike and Duck Creek Road* for the congregation of *St. Mark's Church* in 1908 at a cost of $25,000. One of the sources inadvertently identified the home as being in Evanston, Indiana.[9, 10]

Again in 1908 the brothers designed a two and one-half story home for *J. W. Fritsch* of Fritsch and Hugle, Brokers, Auctioneers, and Expert Appraisers, who were located in the Mercantile Library Building. It was to be built on the south side of Duck Creek on *Hudson Avenue* at a cost $2,700.[11]

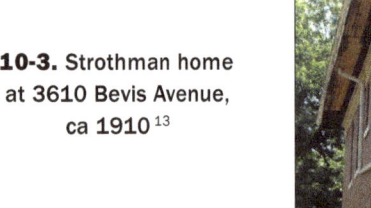

10-3. Strothman home at 3610 Bevis Avenue, ca 1910 [13]

In 1910, the Steinkamps designed a two and one-half story home for *Charles Strothman* on *Bevis Avenue* at a cost of $6,000.[12] The house was just around the corner from Bernard's home on Clarion Avenue.

The brothers designed a *large automobile garage* and machine shop for *A. L. Pachoud* at *3410–3421 Montgomery Road* in 1912.[14] In 1927, they designed a one-story garage for Mr. Pachoud at *3459 Montgomery Road at Blair Avenue* for $20,000.[15] The latter building is no longer standing.

10-4. Pachoud garage at 3410–3421 Montgomery Road, ca. 1912

In 1913, Joseph and Bernard designed a two-story home at *3528 Wabash Avenue* for *Marie Richter*.[16] The house was demolished for the construction of I-71.

When the *A.S. Boyle Company*—makers of "Old English" floor wax—relocated from the office and store the brothers had designed in 1904 on W. Eighth Street to Evanston in 1913, Joseph and Bernard were charged with the design of a new two-story manufacturing facility to cost $30,000. The factory was to be located on the north side of *Langdon (Dana) Avenue* near Montgomery Avenue, and there were plans to link it to the Norfolk and Western railroad.[17, 18] The following June, the *Cincinnati Enquirer* reported that the A.S. Boyle Company was planning a three-story factory building north of Langdon between Bevis and Wabash Avenues, at a cost of $20,000.[19] Currently, at 1940 Dana Avenue there is a two-story store and factory at this site.

10-5. Ad for Old English Floor Wax [20]

10-6. A.S. Boyle Company, 1949 Dana Avenue, ca. 1913

In 1914, Joseph and Bernard drew up plans for a one-story *photo-play house* at *Montgomery Road and Dana Avenue* for *Andrew Niedenthal*.[21] It was to be Evanston's first motion picture house and cost $15,000. The seating was listed as 350–380. On December 23, 1950, the Veterans of Foreign Wars hosted a party for 1000 neighborhood children at the theater.[22] The theater closed shortly afterward and was later demolished.[23]

10-7. Evanston Theater, ca. 1914 [23]

When it was planned in 1914, *St. Mark's Catholic Church* was hailed as a new type of church. It was in the Roman basilica style and a new type of structure for Cincinnati, with the bell tower separate from the church proper.[24,25] The architects for the building were listed as H.J. Schlacks of Chicago and Joseph Steinkamp and Brother (as associate architects), and the cost has been reported to be between $100,000 and $150,000.[26-29] The cornerstone for the church was laid on November 29, 1914, at the corner of

Montgomery Road and Jonathon Avenue in Evanston. The ceremony followed a parade and was presided over by Monsignor John B. Murry.[29] The new church was dedicated in June of 1916 by Archbishop Moeller following a parade of 8,000 men representing Catholic congregations and societies. B. T. [sic] Steinkamp was listed as a member of the planning committee.[30] The parish was staffed by members of the Missionaries of the Precious Blood from the very beginning. Originally a predominantly German-American community, the parish began to change with the construction of Interstate 71 and the consequent movement of many people from this part of the city to the suburbs. For many years, it was one of the most vibrant African American Catholic Communities. Because of the declining number of parishioners, St. Mark's closed in 2010.[31]

10-8. St Mark's Church, 3500 Montgomery Road, ca. 1916

In April 1922, *St. Mark's Parochial School* was destroyed by fire, with the loss estimated at $67,000.[32] The following month, Joseph and Bernard were completing plans for a new building on the site of the previous school, to cost $125,000. In addition to the school facilities, it would have an auditorium and a lunchroom with a capacity for 900 students.[33, 34] The Architectural Record incorrectly identified the school as being in Evanston, IL, but later corrected the mistake.[35, 36]

10-9. St. Mark's Parochial School, ca. 1924 [35]

The brothers drew up plans to alter a building owned by *Albert Frey* on the corner of *Woodburn and Gilpin Avenues* to convert it to a flat building in 1923.[37] This section of Woodburn has recently undergone considerable redevelopment and the flat has been replaced by upscale condominiums.

The Steinkamps designed a home for *Edward J. Smith* at 2003 *Crane Avenue* in 1933.[38]

10-10. Smith home at 2003 Crane Avenue, ca. 1933 [39]

CHAPTER 11

Anderson and Mariemont

In July 1936, Joseph and Bernard sought a modification to the building code to erect a two-story addition for the *Elstun Theater* on *Beechmont Avenue* at the corner of *Plymouth Avenue,* in Anderson.[1] However, the theater was actually constructed a short distance away from Plymouth Avenue, at 2231–33 Beechmont Avenue in Mount Washington. General contractor J.C. Frazer directed the construction.

11-1. Sketch of Elstun Theater, ca. 1936 [2]

Mrs. Rose E. Dodge was the owner of the theater, and her son, Elstun Dodge, was the manager.[2] The theater featured a single screen, air conditioning, and parking at the rear of the building. Originally it had seating for 485 patrons, but it was expanded to 800 seats in 1945.[4] The theater was dedicated in ceremonies on October 16, 1937, at which Cincinnati Mayor Russell Wilson was the guest speaker.[5] The theater closed in the early 1960s, and the facility was used as a furniture store, Furniture Fashions, shortly afterwards. The building burned as a result of arson in 1992 and was demolished in 1995.[6] There is no record of the Steinkamps being involved with other construction in the Anderson area.

Around 1923, *Charles Livingood* selected Joseph G. Steinkamp and Brother to design a massive Tudor-style block on the main square of *Mariemont,* opposite the Mariemont Inn, to be known as the *Theater Block*. It was said to be designed after the Rows of Chester, England, and was to be the principal structure in the village.[7]

11-2. Elstun Theater, ca. 1958 [3]

11-3. Mariemont Theater Block, ca. 1926 [8]

However, in 1926, several architects, including the brothers, were let go and the block was never built. In *John Nolen and Mariemont: Building a New Town in Ohio*, Rogers states, "It is unfortunate that Steinkamp's imposing four-story range of shops, offices, apartments, and theater with an arcaded walk was never executed. Its monumental and elegant bulk would have balanced the Mariemont Inn...."[9] One can only imagine how magnificent this enormous structure would have been, sitting across the Mariemont square from the Inn and the National Exemplar Restaurant.

11-4. The Rows of Chester, England [10]

This was not Joseph's only contact with Mariemont. The town of Mariemont, founded by philanthropist Mary Emery, was actually named after one of her family's summer homes. This home was in Middletown, Rhode Island, and was named after a town in England.[11] Middletown is next to Rhode Island's more famous retreat for the rich and famous, Newport. The Emerys would take their private train car to southern Rhode Island and then another train and ferry to Middletown. Joseph is reported to have helped with some of the designs for renovations of their Middletown summer home.[12]

CHAPTER 12

Other Ohio Cities

Johann (J.B.) Steinkamp and the Steinkamp brothers are credited with several buildings in locations in Ohio, but also outside of Cincinnati proper, from Toledo to Fayetteville and several places in between.

Toledo

As early as 1888, J. B. Steinkamp designed two stores and two flats, each of four stories, and two large dwellings of three stories in *Toledo* for *Thomas Emery's Sons*. The total cost of all the structures was reported to be $30,000, which would be over $800,000 today.[1]

Hartwell

J. B. Steinkamp designed a 5-story store and flat at the corner of *Vine and Mary Streets* for *H. E. Miners* in 1888 that cost $9,000.[2] The building is no longer standing.

Hamilton

Working alone after his father's death, Joseph designed a shingle house for *Joseph W. Doron* in 1889 in *Prospect Hill* in Hamilton, Ohio.[3] Later, in 1906, the brothers worked with Mr. Doron and designed the *Dorona Flats* on *High Street* in the Second Renaissance

12-1. Joseph Doron House, ca. 1889 [5]

Revival style. At the time, it was one of the prominent apartment buildings in the city.[4, 5] The following year, Mr. Doron built the nearby *Verona Flats* in a similar style, but there is no information that links the Steinkamps to the design of that building.[5]

12-2. Dorona Flats, 6 N. Sixth Street, ca. 1907 [6]

Fayetteville

In 1906, the Steinkamp brothers designed a school and dormitory for the *St. Aloysius Academy* for the *Sisters of Charity* in Fayetteville at a cost of $25,000.[7, 8]

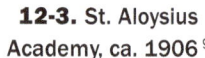
12-3. St. Aloysius Academy, ca. 1906 [9]

Milford

The same year, the brothers designed a one and one-half story, five-room *frame bungalow* for *John B. Krusling* of Terrace Park.[10]

Cheviot

Still in 1906, the brothers designed a seven-room *brick home* for *Henry Kenkel* at a cost of $4,000.[11]

Also, in Cheviot, the Steinkamps designed a *two-story store* for *Mr. John Wahl* in 1906.[12]

Oxford

The *Tallawanda Apartments* were built for *Miami University* faculty in 1908 and designed by Joseph Steinkamp in the second Renaissance Revival style. Miami University leased the building for students and faculty housing before purchasing it in 1952, when it was converted to a women's residence hall. The three-story brick building originally included a community dining room for its residents. In 1929, a restaurant called "Tuffy's" opened in the basement and served its famous toasted rolls until 1973. Tuffy's toasted rolls have become a Miami tradition and are still available at Miami University. Unfortunately, the apartment building was demolished in 1984.[13,14]

12-4. Tallawanda Apartments, ca. 1908 [14]

Lima

In 1909, the brothers designed an *apartment building* containing six apartments of six rooms each for *G. L. Hackman*.[15]

Deer Park

The Steinkamps were designing a brick and concrete, one-story, four-room school for St. John's Parish in 1923.[16, 17]

12-5. St. John's School, 7121 Plainfield Road, ca. 1923 [18]

Norwood

In 1900, Joseph and Bernard designed a two-story hospital building for the *Sisters of Charity* in Norwood.[19]

In 1908, they designed an addition to the *St. Joseph Orphan Asylum* at a cost of $4,000.[20, 21]

The brothers designed a two and one-half brick residence for the company of *Fritsch and Hugle* on the corner of *Forest and Jefferson Avenues* in 1904.[22] Joseph Fritsch and William Hugle were real estate brokers who had their office in the Mercantile Library Building.[23]

12-6. 4171 Forest Avenue, ca. 1904 [24]

The Steinkamps' only other work in Norwood consisted of a building with four apartments for *Anton Kramer* on *Mill Avenue* in 1914.[25]

Wyoming

The brothers designed a two and one-half story colonial home for *Mrs. Max Mueller* at *308 Elm Avenue* in Wyoming in 1910.[26, 27]

Dayton

St. Mary's Catholic Church hired Joseph and Bernard to design a new *two-story school* at Xenia and Allen Streets in Dayton in 1913/1914 at a cost of $50,000.[28, 29] At that time, their bother, the Reverend George Steinkamp, was the assistant pastor.

Another Catholic school designed by Joseph and Bernard in Dayton was *St. John's Catholic School* on the corner of *Williams and Hartford Streets* in 1923.[30] The article reported that Reverend Steinkamp was the pastor of St. John's at that time.

In May of 1930, *The Dayton Daily News* reported "Very prominent architects help design church."[31] The Steinkamp brothers designed *Our Lady of Mercy Church* in Dayton. George was the pastor of this church from 1928 to 1933.[32]

Franklin

The brothers designed a hotel and picture theater complex in Franklin, Ohio, in May of 1914. It was for *Mr. E. J. Haberer* (or Heberer) of the *Franklin Hotel Company* and the cost was put at $25,000.[33, 34] However, later in August of the same year it was reported that the project was postponed indefinitely.[35] It turns out that the project was postponed because Mr. Haberer was in jail at the time. Seems he was a con artist who had bilked a local hotel where he was staying of a tidy sum of money for his room and board while promoting the grand hotel he was going to build.[36]

Cummingsville and South Cummingsville

Another noted Cincinnati architect, Henry Siter, designed the original building in the photo below for the *Garfield Public School* in 1905 in South Cummingsville, and the Steinkamps designed an addition to the school on the left side in 1927. The older, principal wing is an excellent example of the eclectic blending of the Second Renaissance Revival, Queen Anne, and Romanesque Revival styles in a large public building.[37] The Steinkamps remodeled the entire building and added a gymnasium, auditorium, two classrooms, and a kindergarten.[38]

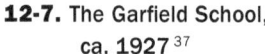

12-7. The Garfield School, ca. 1927 [37]

Joseph and Bernard designed a *three-story recreation building/bath house* for *St. Joseph's Orphan Asylum* in 1907 at a cost of $25,000.[39, 40] The asylum was located on *Cherry Street near Blue Rock Street* in Cummingsville.[41]

In 1910 the brothers designed a two and one-half story brick home for *H. B. Thien* at *4045 Runnymede Avenue*.[42] The home is no longer standing.

Northside

Joseph and Bernard drew up plans to convert a home at *4233 Langland Avenue* into a two-story apartment for the *Merrill Corporation of Chicago* in 1916 at a cost of $4000.[43]

In 1922, Joseph and Bernard designed a bank building for the *Provident Savings Bank and Trust Company* in Northside at the corner of *Hamilton Avenue and Knowlton Street*.[44] Bernard H. Kroger, founder of the Kroger chain of supermarkets, was the president of the bank.

12-8. Provident Savings Bank and Trust Company, 4140 Hamilton Avenue, ca. 1922 [45]

Winton Place

In 1908, the brothers designed a two-story *brick factory and flat* on the corner of Clifton and Spring Grove Avenues for *M. B. Farrin* at a cost of $15,000.[46]

The Steinkamps designed a one-story truck garage for the *B. H. Wess Grain and Coal Company* on *Durham Avenue* in 1919.[47]

Lockland

After the barns at *St. Rita School for the Deaf* on *Canal Road* in Lockland were destroyed by fire in 1919, Joseph and Bernard offered their services without charge to design replacements that cost between $10,000 and $15,000.[48, 49]

Pleasant Ridge

Joseph and Bernard designed a home for *Mr. A.D. Roessler* at *2648 Briarcliff [sic] Avenue* in 1933.[50, 51] It may have been *2650 Briarcliffe Avenue* for *Mr. A. B. Roessler*, a prominent Cincinnati lawyer. However, his own residence was on Terrance Avenue in Clifton.[52] In addition to other errors in the two articles, the July 8th article lists Mr. Roessler's office number the same as that of the brother's office number in the Mercantile Library Building in 1933.[53]

12-9. 2650 Briarcliffe Avenue, ca. 1933

In 1941, Joseph and Bernard designed a four-apartment building on *Lester Road* in Pleasant Ridge for *Bernard*.[54] In July of that year, an ad appeared in the *Cincinnati Enquirer* for the apartment building, indicating that it was built as an investment for Bernard.[55] Just one year later, the building was sold[56], possibly owing to Bernard's poor health at the time.

12-10. Sketch of Lester Road Apartment, ca. 1941 [56]

12-11. Lester Road Apartment

Oakley

In 1907, the *Cincinnati Enquirer* reported that a "Mr. Steinkamp" had secured the *Wefler (Weller?) Grounds Baseball Park* with the plan to tear down the old stands and build new ones behind home plate for the new Oakley Park.[57] "Mr. Steinkamp" appears to be one of the brothers, because the article refers to his connection with the Bismark [sic] Café, which the brothers had designed. For a few years, the fields were known as the "Oakley-Steinkamp's Park."

In 1942, Bernard filed a building permit for a similar four-family apartment at the corner of *28th Street and Robertson Road* in Oakley. The building cost $10,000 and appears to have been another apartment built as an investment property.[58] If indeed they both worked on designing this apartment, it demonstrates that they were still collaborating in 1942. This may have been the last project they worked on together because Bernard passed away in 1943.[59]

12-12. 28th Street and Robertson Road, ca. 1942 [60]

Although its location cannot be verified, *Moving Picture World* reported in 1921 that Joseph Steinkamp was designing a 1,600-seat picture theater at an estimated cost of $60,000 to be built on ***Oakley Square***.[61] Possibly, it was never built, because the time and location do not coincide with any of the theaters around Oakley Square.

CHAPTER 13

Work Outside Ohio

Although the Steinkamp brothers carried out most of their work in Ohio, they occasionally ventured outside its borders. They may have done a considerable amount of work in West Virginia, but it can't be confirmed.

Kentucky

It appears that one of the Steinkamps' few excursions across the Ohio River into Kentucky was to design *The Emery House* on *E. Fifth Street* in Covington, in 1890.[1] It was stated that "Its austere but handsome façade was probably designed by the Steinkamps," and given the timeframe, may have referred to J. B. Steinkamp.

In 1919, they once again crossed the Ohio River and designed a bungalow for Mr. *J. C. Browning* in *Falmouth, Kentucky*.[2]

Several years later, they designed one of at least three stores for the *Kroger Grocery and Baking Company* on *Monmouth Street in Newport, Kentucky* which housed a Pay'n Takit market.[3]

13-1. Emery House, 7 E. Fifth Street, ca. 1890

13-2. Kroger Bakery
708 Monmouth Street,
ca. 1938

Indiana

In 1906, the Steinkamps designed an apartment for *Thomas Emery's Sons* in *New Albany, Indiana,* estimated to cost $150,000.[4, 5]

That same year, their firm designed a three-story addition to a furniture plant for *Hillenbrand & Company* in *Batesville, Indiana*, which may have been for the Batesville Casket Company.[6]

The following year, the brothers designed the *First National Bank Building* in *Batesville*.[7]

13-3. First National Bank Building, ca. 1907 [8]

West Virginia

The brothers designed a three-story apartment building with 12 flats in *Charleston, West Virginia,* for *Mr. Benjamin Baer* in 1910.[9] Mr. Baer was a whisky distiller who had ties with Charleston and Cincinnati. When West Virginia went dry in 1914, he turned to the development of real estate projects.[10] *The Plumbers' Trade Journal* states that this was but one of 12 apartment buildings that "Cincinnati architects" were designing for Mr. Baer in Charleston.[11] The cost of this one was estimated to be $35,000.

Rhode Island

As noted in the chapter on Mariemont, Ohio, in 1913 Joseph had worked on additions and renovations for *Thomas and Mary Emery's* summer home, *Mariemont,* in *Middletown, Rhode Island.*[12]

13-4. Mariemont in Middletown, Rhode Island [13] (photo, Google)

CHAPTER 14

Patents of Joseph G. Steinkamp

In his spare time, Joseph Steinkamp seems to have been an inventor. His name is on two patents as the sole inventor, and he was assigned one-half of another. The three patents could not be more diverse in nature.

June 2, 1903: Patent No. 729, 821: Drinking Trough for Domestic Animals. Jacob F. Weitzel. Assignor of one-half to Joseph G. Steinkamp[1]

What appears to be an unusual invention for architect Joseph is this drinking trough for domestic animals. The only other reference having to do with animals found in the literature on Joseph dealt with building codes in Cincinnati.[2] One-half of this patent was assigned to Joseph by a Mr. Jacob F. Weitzel. Mr. Weitzel, a prolific inventor, registered quite a few patents, especially dealing with sheet metal products.

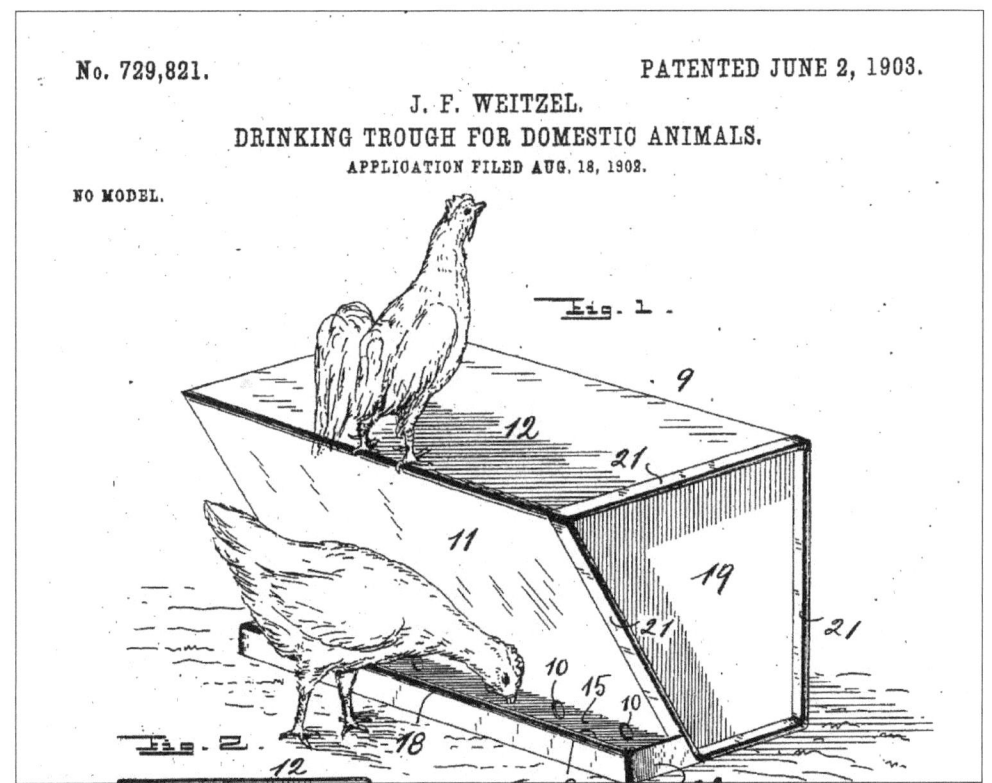

14-1. Drinking Trough for Domestic Animals[1]

September 24, 1907: US 866823: A Cabinet-kitchen (Filed October 29, 1906)[3]

Steinkamp's most practical invention is probably his fold-away kitchen. As Joseph described it, "It is the object of my invention to provide a kitchen for use especially in flats, without the utilization of a separate room therefor, and while providing the usual furniture found in a kitchen yet concentrates the same in a form which is compact and convenient."

To work with the limited space in small flats, the kitchen cabinets would fold over appliances and counters when not in use. This would provide additional living space. When a mother said the kitchen was closed, the kitchen was *really* closed! This design has caught on recently with small apartments and tiny homes, where walls can be rolled or folded to provide alternative living space as needed.[4]

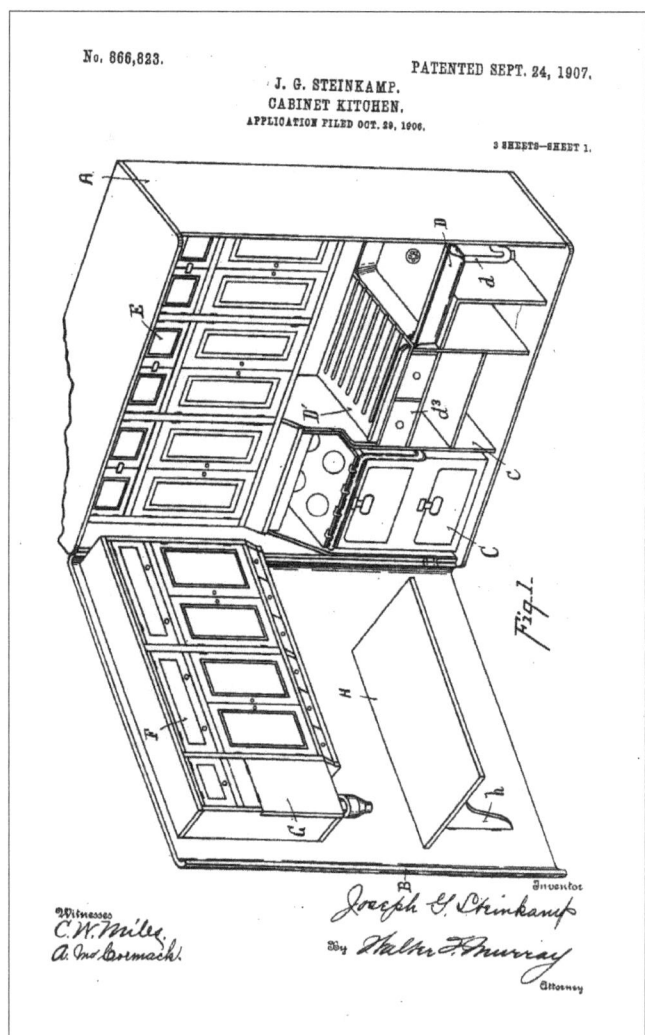

14-2. Cabinet-Kitchen [3]

November 5, 1929: Patent No. 1,734,748: Multi-Control Locking Mechanism (Filed August 29, 1927)[5]

Joseph's third patent came much later and was for "… a locking device adapted to be set by a suitable elapsed time mechanism… for opening or unlocking with a key by the deposit of coins in proportion to the elapsed periods of time." It was basically the forerunner of parking meters.

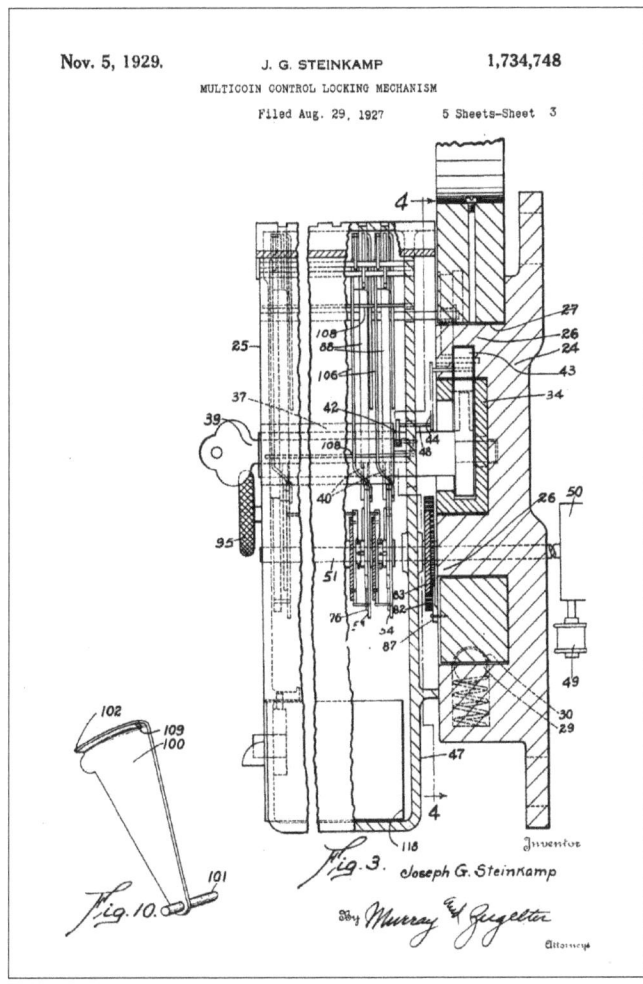

14-3. Multi-Control Locking Mechanism [5]

References

Chapter 1 • Introduction

1. John Patrick Barrett. Electricity at the Columbian Exposition. R.R. Donnelley and Sons. Chicago. 1894 p 165–170.
2. Constance J. Moore and Nancy M. Broermann. Maria Longworth Storer: From Music and Art to Popes and Presidents. University of Cincinnati Press. Cincinnati. 2019 p 86.
3. Centennial Exposition of the Ohio Valley and Central States. https://americasbesthistory.com/wfcincinnati1888.html.
4. Ohio History Central. http://www.ohiohistorycentral.org/w/Cincinnati,_Ohio.
5. C. F. Goss. Cincinnati, the Queen City, 1788–1912. S.J. Clarke Publishing Company. Chicago, Cincinnati. 1912 p 512.
6. *Williams' Cincinnati Directory.* 1896.
7. Greater Cincinnati and Its People: A History. Lewis A. Leonard, ed. Volume IV. Lewis Historical Publishing Company. New York. 1927 p 595.
8. Sue Ann Painter. Architecture in Cincinnati: An Illustrated History of Designing and Building an American City. Ohio University Press. Athens, Ohio. 2006 p 61.
9. Walter E. Langsam and Alice Weston. Biographical Dictionary of Cincinnati Architects, 1788–1940. Architectural Foundation of Cincinnati. Cincinnati, Ohio. 2008.
10. *Cincinnati Enquirer.* April 13, 1924 p 64.
11. *Williams' Cincinnati Directory.* 1905.
12. *The Western Architect and Builder.* Volume 21, No. 17 1904 p 3.
13. *Williams' Cincinnati Directory.* 1930.
14. _____. 1945.
15. United States Department of the Interior. National Park Service, National Register of Historic Places Registration Form. The Somerset Apartments. May 8, 2014. Section 8, p 13.
16. Annual Reports of the City Departments of the City of Cincinnati for the Fiscal Year Ending December 31, 1875. Fifth Annual Report of the Clerk Office. University of Cincinnati. December 31, 1875 p 824.
17. *Cincinnati Magazine.* "Lombardy Flats: The Enduring Charms of a Hannaford Novelty." Greg Hand. August 24, 2018.
18. Millard F. Rogers, Jr. John Nolen and Mariemont: Building a New Town in Ohio. Johns Hopkins University Press. Baltimore, Maryland. 2001 p 175.
19. Klaus Steinkamp. Personal communication.

20. Jeffrey G. Herbert. Old Saint Mary's Church, Cincinnati, Ohio: A History of the First 160 Years of Catholic Faith. Little Miami Publishing Co. 2006 p 116.

21. https://www.givecentral.org/location/1166/event/27085.

22. Cincinnati und sein Deutschthum: eine Geschichte der Entwickelung Cincinnati's und seines Deutschthums, mit biographischen Skizzen und Illustrationen. Queen City Publishing Company. Cincinnati, Ohio. 1901.

23. *Cincinnati Enquirer.* April 19, 1926 p 16.

24. History of Greene County Ohio: Its People, Industries and Institutions. Hon. M.A. Broadstone, Editor-in-Chief. B.F. Bowen & Company, Inc. Indianapolis, Indiana. 1918 p 94 (index).

25. *Williams' Cincinnati Directory.* 1880.

26. Jeffrey G. Herbert. Old Saint Mary's Church, Cincinnati, Ohio: A History of the First 160 Years of Catholic Faith. Little Miami Publishing Co. 2006 p 130.

27. *Cincinnati Enquirer.* December 25, 1921 p 46.

28. Old St. Mary's Church. Used with permission.

29. Memoirs of the Miami Valley. John C. Hover, et al., eds. Volume III. Robert O. Law Company. Chicago. 1920 p 394–395.

30. Greater Cincinnati and Its People: A History. Lewis A. Leonard, ed. Volume IV. Lewis Historical Publishing Company. New York. 1927 p 594.

31. B. La Bree. Notable men of Cincinnati at the beginning of the 20th century (Fetter's notable men of Cincinnati). Geo. G. Fetter Company. Cincinnati. 1903 p 159.

32. Courtesy of the Steinkamp family. Used with permission.

33. *Cincinnati Enquirer.* January 17, 1963 p 23.

34. _____. January 15, 1982 p 32.

35. Robert and Valda Moore. Personal communication.

36. *Cincinnati Enquirer (Kentucky Edition).* April 16, 1927 p 22.

37. *Cincinnati Enquirer.* April 8, 1928 p 50.

38. _____. May 27, 1928 p 54.

39. _____. July 2, 1928 p 18.

40. _____. July 5, 1928 p 16.

41. _____. November 18, 1928 p 48.

42. _____. December 29, 1929 p 40.

43. *Williams' Cincinnati Directory.* 1929.

44. _____. 1934.

45. M. Carol (Steinkamp) Molleran. Personal communication.

46. *Cincinnati Enquirer.* September 25, 1943 p 20.

47. _____. March 18, 1944 p 6.

48. *Williams' Cincinnati Directory.* 1944.

49. *Cincinnati Enquirer.* June 16, 1936 p 24.

50. *Williams' Cincinnati Directory.* 1945.

51. *Cincinnati Enquirer.* July 25, 1941 p 19.

52. _____. April 7, 1942 p 18.

53. _____. October 22, 1948 p 15, p 30.

54. *The New York Times.* October 22, 1948 p 26.

55. *Cincinnati Post.* October 21, 1948 p 30.

56. *Journal Herald (Dayton, Ohio).* October 23, 1948 p 2.

57. *Newark Advocate (Newark, Ohio).* October 22, 1948 p 22.

58. *Cincinnati Enquirer.* October 22, 1948 p 15.

59. C. F. Goss. Cincinnati, the Queen City, 1788–1912. S.J. Clarke Publishing Company. Chicago, Cincinnati. 1912 p 513.

60. *Cincinnati Enquirer.* June 2, 1912 p 19.

61. *The Catholic Telegraph.* Volume LIX, No. 51, 1890-12-1 p 11.

62. *Cincinnati Post.* September 23, 1913 p 2.

63. _____. March 18, 1915 p 2.

64. *Cincinnati Enquirer.* Change may be suggested: In Safety Zone Ordinance-Club Hears Many Protests. July 16, 1924 p 4.

65. Memoirs of the Miami Valley. John C. Hover, et al., eds. Volume III. Robert O. Law Company. Chicago, Illinois. 1920 p 395.

66. *Ft. Lauderdale News.* March 30, 1930 p 3.

67. Court of Common Pleas, County of Hamilton, State of Ohio. No. A-81062. August 31, 1942.

68. *Cincinnati Enquirer.* October 31, 1908 p 8.

69. _____. May 15, 1909 p 8.

70. Court of Common Pleas, County of Hamilton, State of Ohio. No. A-81062. May 7, 1943.

71. Ohio Department of Health. Certificate of Death. March 1944.

72. *Cincinnati Enquirer.* June 15, 1943 p 3.

73. *Cincinnati Post.* January 18, 1922 p 3.

74. *Cincinnati Enquirer.* "50 Years Ago Today." October 17, 1961 p 11.

75. *American Art Directory.* Volume 11 1914 p 283.

76. *The Western Architect and Builder.* Volume 25, No. 4 1908 p 8.

77. *Cincinnati Enquirer.* October 31, 1908 p 8.

78. *The Ohio Architect & Builder.* Volume XXV, No. 5 1915 p 31.

79. *American Art Annual.* Volume XVII 1920 p 197.

80. *Indianapolis Journal.* Volume 52, No. 218. August 6, 1902 p 3.

81. *Cincinnati Enquirer.* October 21, 1908 p 8.

82. _____. May 15, 1909 p 8.

83. *The Western Architect and Builder.* Volume 25, No. 17 1908 p 7.

84. _____. Volume 23, No. 52 1906 p 614.

85. *The American Contractor.* Volume 35, No. 27 1914 p 85.

86. *Cincinnati Enquirer.* July 10, 1914 p 15.

87. *Building Management.* July 1913 p 78–82.

88. Elementary Civics. McCarthy C, Swan F, Willing J. Thompson, Brown & Company. New York. 1916 p 213–214.

89. *American Beacon Journal (Akron, Ohio).* October 21, 1913 p 10.

90. *Cincinnati Enquirer.* "Delegates Are Named." April 16, 1924 p 10.

91. _____. "Apartment Plans Approved By Expert Named By Court." June 14, 1924 p 14.

92. _____. April 20, 1925 p 8.

93. _____. April 29, 1930 p 10.

94. *The Xaverian News.* January 14, 1931 p 1.

95. *Cincinnati Enquirer.* "Proposes Two Plans." January 24, 1932 p 17.

96. _____. "Meeting Hears Of Plans." April 5, 1932 p 6.

97. _____. February 10, 1932 p 20.

98. _____. January 26, 1933 p 10.

99. _____. October 27, 1935 p 37.

100. _____. "Three Veteran Architects Honored." February 28, 1940 p 12.

101. _____. "Architects Give Honor to Joseph G. Steinkamp." July 4, 1941 p 42.

102. Greater Cincinnati and Its People: A History. Lewis A. Leonard, ed. Volume IV. Lewis Historical Publishing Company. New York. 1927. p 596.

103. Ohio Architect and Builder. "Cincinnati, Queen City of the Central West." Volume XIII, No. 6 1909 pp 9-25.

104. *Williams' Cincinnati Directory.* 1902.

105. _____. 1908.

106. *Cincinnati Enquirer.* September 25, 1943 p 20.

107. _____. September 26, 1943 p 31.

108. _____. May 27, 1969 p 40.

109. *The Ohio Architect & Builder.* Volume 3, No. 2 1904 p 51.

110. *Cincinnati Enquirer.* February 9, 1907 p 10.

111. _____. April 25, 1909 p 13.

112. _____. July 31, 1910 p 37.

113. _____. September 25, 1912 p 13.

114. _____. "Mirth Greets Stunt Night." April 2, 1930 p 12.

115. *Cincinnati Enquirer.* May 14, 1935 p 7.

116. _____. "Housing Officials On Alert To Reduce Insurance Rates; Strict Inspection Required." April 19, 1936 p 4.

117. _____. February 6, 1936 p 23.

118. _____. February 7, 1936 p 23.

119. https://www.linkedin.com/in/mark-steinkamp-28a81632.

120. *Cincinnati Enquirer.* November 4, 2018 p A28.

121. _____. April 3, 2009 p 16.

122. Architectural Foundation of Cincinnati. www.architecturecincy.org.

123. *Cincinnati Enquirer.* February 19, 1960 p 46.

124. *The Catholic Telegraph.* 1909-06 p 2.

125. History of Greene County Ohio: Its People, Industries and Institutions. Hon. M.A. Broadstone, Editor-in-Chief. B.F. Bowen & Company, Inc. Indianapolis, Indiana. 1918 p 140.

126. *The Dayton Daily News.* June 18, 1933 p 7.

127. *The American Contractor.* Volume 34, No. 35 1913 p 65.

128. _____. Volume 35, No. 14 1914 p 95.

129. *The Dayton Daily News.* November 27, 1923 p 2.

130. _____. December 3, 1923 p 11.

131. _____. "Very Prominent Architects Help Design Church." May 18, 1930 p 21.

132. *The Journal Herald (Dayton, Ohio).* December 2, 1961.

133. *Cincinnati Enquirer.* June 20, 1926 p 87.

134. _____. November 15, 1936 p 8.

135. *The Dayton Daily News.* June 19, 1933 p 6.

136. _____. April 20, 1943 p 16.

137. *Cincinnati Enquirer.* December 4, 1961 p 33.

138. _____. December 5, 1943 p 39.

139. _____. April 12, 1951 p 30.

140. *Cincinnati Post.* February 25, 1931 p 18.

Chapter 2 • Downtown

1. C. F. Goss. Cincinnati, the Queen City, 1788–1912. S.J. Clarke Publishing Company. Chicago, Cincinnati. 1912 p 512.

2. http://www.cincinnativiews.net/downtown_streets.htm.

3. U.S. Department of the Interior. National Park Service. National Register of Historic Places. Inventory-Nomination Form: Emery Row: 1985. Item number 8, p 5.

4. Walter E. Langsam. Biographical Dictionary of Cincinnati Architects, 1788–1940. Susannah Sachdeva and Sue Ann Painter, eds. Architectural Foundation of Cincinnati. Cincinnati, Ohio. 2008.

5. *Cincinnati Enquirer*. February 8, 1882 p 8.

6. National Register of Historic Places. www.ohiohistory.org.

7. Historic Hotels of America. The Cincinnatian Hotel. https://www.historichotels.org/hotels-resorts/the-cincinnatian-hotel/.

8. The Palace Hotel. http://cincinnativiews.net/images-3/Palace%20Hotel.jpg

9. The Cincinnatian Hotel. guestreservations.com.

10. The Somerset Apartments. National Register of Historic Places Registration Form. https://www.nps.gov/nr/feature/places/pdfs/14000355.pdf.

11. *Cincinnati Enquirer*. September 11, 1882 p 7.

12. _____. February 11, 1892 p 12.

13. *The Inland Architect and News Record*. Volume XI, No. 10 1887 p 100.

14. *Williams' Cincinnati Directory*. 1890.

15. _____. Volume XII, No. 2 1888 p 19.

16. *Williams' Cincinnati Directory*. 1884.

17. *Architecture and Building: A Journal of Investment and Construction*. "Building (News Supplement)." Volume X, No. 17 1889 p 2.

18. *Williams' Cincinnati Directory*. 1889.

19. *Architecture and Building: A Journal of Investment and Construction*. "Building (News Supplement)." Volume X, No. 12 1889 p 2.

20. *Williams' Cincinnati Directory*. 1890.

21. Waldo Apartments. https://waldoapartments.com/.

22. *Ohio Architect and Builder*. "Cincinnati, Queen City of the West." Volume XIII, No. 6 1909 p 8.

23. Queen City Survey: Observations and Overviews of Cincinnati. Best places to experience the architecture of Joseph & Benjamin Steinkamp in Cincinnati. January 22, 2008.

24. *Williams' Cincinnati Directory*. 1890.

25. *The Ohio Architect and Builder*. Volume 13, No. 6 1909 p14.

26. *Cincinnati Enquirer*. April 7, 1894 p 5.

27. _____. September 22, 1935 p 39.

28. *Ohio Architect and Builder*. "Cincinnati, Queen City of the Central West." Volume XIII, No. 6 1909 p 15.

29. *Cincinnati Enquirer*. March 6, 1892 p 2.

30. https://www.hcauditor.org/vintagephotos.asp.

31. *The Inland Architect and News Record*. Volume XIX, No. 3 1892 p 42.

32. https://cincinnatisouthernrailway.org/about/edward-ferguson.php.

33. *Cincinnati Enquirer*. March 19, 1912 p 13.

34. _____. July 29, 1893 p 16.

35. *The American Architect and Building News*. Volume XLI, No. 921 1893 p xv.

36. *Xavier University Newswire*. Xavier student newspaper. 1454. 1930. http://www.exhibit.xavier.edu/student_newspaper/1454.

37. Cincinnati Museum Center History Library and Archives-Pending

38. *The Inland Architect and News Record*. Volume XXI, No. 3 1893 p 42.

39. *Williams' Cincinnati Directory*. 1900.

40. *Cincinnati Enquirer*. April 29, 1941 p 4.

41. *The Inland Architect and News Record*. Volume XXV, No. 6 1895 p 64.

42. *Cincinnati Enquirer*. January 28, 1945 p 36.

43. *The American Architect and Building News*. Volume 56, No. 1115 1897 p xvii.

44. *Cincinnati Enquirer*. October 28, 1900 p 21.

45. "Christopher Sandheger: Germany's Gift to Cincinnati." November 6, 2013. http://pre-prowhiskeymen.blogspot.com/2013/11/christopher-sandheger-germanys-gift-to_6.html.

46. National Register of Historic Places. http://nr.ohpo.org/.

47. http://nr.ohpo.org/Details.aspx?refnum=84001046.

48. *Cincinnati Enquirer*. June 30, 1902 p 5.

49. _____. June 6, 1903 p5.

50. https://mercantilelibrary.com/about-us/.

51. *WVXU, Cincinnati Public Radio*. Mercantile library building granted local historic landmark designation. https://www.wvxu.org/post/mercantile-library-building-granted-local-historic-landmark-designation#stream/0. February 18, 2021.

52. http://www.cincinnativiews.net/buildings_7.htm. photo.

53. *The Ohio Architect & Builder*. Volume 3. No. 2 1904 p 51.

54. http://www.cincinnativiews.net/.htm.

55. *The Ohio Architect and Builder*. Volume 3, No. 2 1904, p 49.

56. *Williams' Cincinnati Directory*. 1908.

57. *Cincinnati Enquirer.* April 23, 1913, p13.
58. *The Western Architect and Builder.* Volume 21, No. 46 1904 p 2.
59. Hombach & Groene. Sterling Glass Company, 1069 Celestial Place, Mount Adams. Rombach & Groene Collection (SC296-1034). Cincinnati Museum Center History Library and Archives. Used with permission.
60. *Cincinnati Post.* August 17, 1904 p 2.
61. *The Western Architect and Builder.* Volume 21, No. 30 1904 p 3.
62. *Williams' Cincinnati Directory.* 1906.
63. Courtesy of Hamilton County Auditor Dusty Rhodes. Parcel Number: 075-0002-0126-00.
64. *The Western Architect and Builder.* Volume 21 1904 p 215.
65. _____. Volume 21, No. 22 1904 p 3.
66. *Williams' Cincinnati Directory.* 1910.
67. *Cincinnati Enquirer.* November 17, 1908 p 2.
68. *The Western Architect and Builder.* Volume 21, No. 37 1904 p 2.
69. *The Ohio Architect and Builder.* Volume 3, No. 5 1904 p 54.
70. http://cincinnatihistorichomes.com/neighborhoods/dayton-street/.
71. *The Ohio Architect & Builder.* Volume 3. No. 3 1904 p 55.
72. *The Engineering Record.* Volume 51, No. 10 1905 p 45.
73. *Cincinnati Enquirer.* May 4, 1909 p 5.
74. http://www.gregwrightandsons.com/aboutus.htm.
75. *Engineering News.* Volume LIII, No. 23 1905 p 219.
76. *Williams' Cincinnati Directory.* 1906.
77. *Cincinnati Post.* November 23, 1938 p 4.
78. https://www.britannica.com/topic/Kroger-Co
79. G. Laycock. The Kroger story: a century of innovation. The Kroger Company. Cincinnati, Ohio. 1983 p 36.
80. *Engineering News.* Volume 54, No. 5 1905 p 39.
81. *Williams' Cincinnati Directory.* 1905.
82. *The Western Architect and Builder.* Volume 23, 1906 p 222.
83. Hamilton County Auditor. Parcel Number: 084-0002-0047-00.
84. *The Western Architect and Builder.* Volume 25, No. 24 1906 p 6.
85. _____. Volume 24, No. 22 1907 p 2.
86. *Cincinnati Enquirer.* November 26, 1907 p 7.
87. *The Ohio Architect and Builder.* Volume 11, No. 4 1908 p 68.
88. *American Architect and Building News.* Volume 93, No. 1684 1908 p 20.

89. *The Western Architect and Builder.* Volume 24, No. 25 1907 p 2.
90. *Williams' Cincinnati Directory.* 1909.
91. *The Western Architect and Builder.* Volume 24, No. 22 1907 p 2.
92. *Cincinnati Enquirer.* March 6, 1927 p 58.
93. *The Ohio Architect and Builder.* Volume 10, No. 5 1907 p 62.
94. *The Western Architect and Builder.* Volume 24, No. 43 1907 p 2.
95. *Williams' Cincinnati Directory.* 1907.
96. *The Ohio Architect and Builder.* Volume 9, No. 8 1907 p 63.
97. *The Western Architect and Builder.* Volume 24, No. 25 1907 p 2.
98. *Cincinnati Enquirer.* March 8, 1906 p 3.
99. *The Ohio Architect and Builder.* Volume 10. No. 2 1907 p 52.
100. *The Western Architect and Builder.* Volume 25, No. 31 1908 p 2.
101. *Williams' Cincinnati Directory.* 1908.
102. *The Western Architect and Builder.* Volume 25, No. 1 1908 p 3.
103. _____. Volume 25. No. 39 1908 p 2.
104. *Cincinnati Enquirer.* October 25, 1908 p 12.
105. *The Western Architect and Builder.* Volume 25, No. 44 1908 p 3.
106. _____. Volume 25, No. 9 1908 p 3.
107. http://otrmatters.com/over-the-rhine-streets-of-yesteryear/.
108. *The Western Architect and Builder.* Volume 24, No. 42 1908 p 2.
109. *Cincinnati Enquirer.* May 4, 1909 p 5.
110. _____. April 10, 1912 p 15.
111. _____. April 12, 1912 p 12.
112. _____. January 17, 1915, p 27.
113. *Williams' Cincinnati Directory.* 1915.
114. https://www.xavier.edu/mission-identity/xaviers-mission/buildings-statues-and-beauty/andrew-j-and-mary-mcdonald-memorial-library.
115. *The Western Architect and Builder.* Volume 26, No. 25 1909 p 5.
116. *The Engineering Record.* Volume 59, No. 15 1909 p 42a.
117. *The Western Architect and Builder.* Volume 26, No. 8 1909 p 2.
118. *Engineering News.* Volume 53, No. 2 1905 p 12.
119. *The American Contractor.* Volume 37, No. 26 1916 p 84.
120. https://www.bizjournals.com/cincinnati/news/2013/10/01/columbus-developer-to-build-apartments.html

121. *The Catholic Telegraph.* Volume LXVII, No. 22 1909-06-03.
122. *Williams' Cincinnati Directory.* 1902.
123. *The Western Architect and Builder.* Volume 26, No. 24 1909 p 6.
124. *Cincinnati Enquirer.* May 4, 1909 p 5.
125. *The Engineering Record.* Volume 51, No. 10 1905 p 45.
126. *Cincinnati Post.* August 23, 1909 p 7.
127. *Cincinnati Enquirer.* August 21, 1909 p 10.
128. *The Western Architect and Builder.* Volume 26, No. 38 1909 p 5.
129. *Cincinnati Enquirer.* August 22, 1924 p 2.
130. _____. September 24, 1909 p 13.
131. _____. October 1, 1924 p 17.
132. *The Western Architect and Builder.* Volume 26, No. 52 1909 p 4. 312–314.
133. _____. Volume 26, No. 38 1909 p5.
134. *Cincinnati Enquirer.* March 2, 1910 p 13.
135. _____. May 23, 1909 p 19.
136. *Industrial World.* Volume 44, No. 2 1910 p iii.
137. https://silo.tips/download/cincinnati-609-walnut-st.
138. http://www.cincinnativiews.net/other_hotels.htm.
139. https://www.historichotels.org/us/hotels-resorts/21c-museum-hotel-cincinnati-by-mgallery/history.php.
140. National Register of Historic Places. http://nr.ohpo.org/
141. https://www.21cmuseumhotels.com/blog/2013/21c-cincinnati-honored-at-uli-2013-global-awards-for-excellence/.
142. https://www.booking.com/hotel/us/museumcincinnati.html.
143. https://npgallery.nps.gov/NRHP/AssetDetail?assetID=7936597c-bc1d-4eb7-8841-9492fa692f97.
144. *Cincinnati Enquirer.* September 25, 1912 p 13.
145. *Industrial World.* Volume 47, No. 1 1913 p 609.
146. _____. Volume 44, No. 2 1910 p iii.
147. National Register of Historic Places. http://nr.ohpo.org/.
148. https://cincinnati-transit.net/summer2002-3.html .
149. *Cincinnati Enquirer.* August 15, 1914 p 16.
150. *Industrial World.* August 24, 1914 p 1027.
151. *Cincinnati Enquirer.* July 24, 1914 p 13.
152. *The American Contractor.* Volume 35, No. 36 1914 p 77.

153. https://overtherhine.wordpress.com/2012/05/24/the-gradual-hollowing-out-of-urban-cincinnati/.

154. *Cincinnati Enquirer.* October 9, 1914 p 13.

155. *The Ohio Architect, Engineer and Builder.* Volume XXVI, No. 5 1915 p 88.

156. *Cincinnati Enquirer.* September 11, 1915 p 10.

157. *The Construction Record.* Volume 54, No. 13 1915 p 16.

158. *The American Contractor.* Volume. 37, No. 11 1916 p 27.

159. _____. Volume 37, No. 18 1916 p 95.

160. _____. Volume 36, No. 23 1915 p 83.

161. https://knowtheatre.com/.

162. Courtesy of Hamilton County Auditor Dusty Rhodes. Parcel Number: 076-0002-0084-00.

163. *The American Contractor.* Volume 36, No. 5 1915 p 23.

164. *Ice and Refrigeration.* Volume 48, No. 2 1915 p 113.

165. *The American Contractor.* Volume 37, No. 11 1916 p 27.

166. *Motor Age.* Volume XXIX, No. 1 1916 p 43.

167. *Auto Trade Journal.* September 1916 p 176.

168. *The American Contractor.* Volume 38, No. 24 1917 p 24.

169. _____. Volume 38, 1917 p 65, 70.

170. *Cincinnati Enquirer.* March 26, 1917 p 4.

171. *The American Contractor.* Volume 38, No. 15 1917 p 63.

172. Queen City Tour 2012. http://queencitytour.blogspot.com/2012/07/barlow-motors-building.html.

173. Courtesy Archives and Rare Books Library, University of Cincinnati. Used with permission.

174. *The American Contractor.* Volume 39, No. 14 1918 p 70.

175. *Williams' Cincinnati Directory.* 1908.

176. *The American Contractor.* Volume 38, No. 45 1919 p 48.

177. http://www.cincinnativiews.net/images-3/1923%20Auto%20Dealers.jpg.

178. *The American Contractor.* Volume 40, No. 40 1919 p 68.

179. *Cincinnati Enquirer.* June 12, 1921 p 70.

180. Digging Cincinnati History. http://www.diggingcincinnati.com/2012/06/.

181. Leading Manufacturers and Merchants of Cincinnati and Environs: The Great Railroad Centre of the South and Southwest. Illustrated. International Publishing Company. New York. 1886 p 72.

182. *Cincinnati Post.* December 17, 1951 p 21.

183. *The Hotel Monthly.* Volume 27, No. 316 July 1919 p 35.

184. *The American Contractor.* Volume 42, No. 14 1921 p 70.

185. _____. Volume 41, No. 11 1920 p 63.

186. *Cincinnati Post.* January 30, 1907 p 1.

187. _____. December 24, 1902 p 8.

188. *The American Contractor.* Volume 41, No. 29 1920 p 63A.

189. _____. Volume 41, No. 27 1920 p 64.

190. *Cincinnati Enquirer.* July 7, 1921 p 8.

191. _____. August 8, 1920 p 41.

192. _____. February 17, 1929 p 10.

193. *Williams' Cincinnati Directory.* 1922.

194. *Build Management.* Volume XIII, No. 6 1913 p 92.

195. *The American Contractor.* Volume 43, No. 40 1921 p 63.

196. https://historicplaces.net/monument/ohio-national-guard-armory-cincinnati-ohio/AODAwMDMwNjk=/.

197. *Cincinnati Enquirer.* February 3, 1927 p 21.

198. *The Building Witness.* Volume 40, No. 4 1923 p 6.

199. *Cincinnati Enquirer.* September 2, 1923 p13.

200. *Cincinnati Post.* October 8, 1927 p 10.

201. *Cincinnati Enquirer.* January 1, 1928 p 37.

202. *Journal of the American Pharmaceutical Association.* Volume 44, No. 1 January/February 2004 p 21.

203. https://www.smithsonianmag.com/us-history/empire-state-building-1929-31-180957195/.

204. Cincinnati Post. October 8, 1927 p 10.

205. Courtesy of the family of Dr. J.H. Beal. Used with permission.

206. *The American Architect.* August 5, 1929 p 153.

207. Photograph by J. Miles Wolf © 2020. Used with permission.

208. *Cincinnati Post* (online edition). October 10, 2003.

209. *Cincinnati Enquirer.* November 18, 1928 p 15.

210. D. Weise. Used with permission.

211. Phil Armstrong. Used with permission.

212. _____. September 5, 2004 p H1-2.

213. *Cincinnati Enquirer.* March 10, 1937 p 24.

214. _____. April 11, 1937 p 2.

215. _____. November 4, 1939 p 23.

216. *Cincinnati Enquirer.* April 23, 1937 p 20.

217. _____. June 20, 1937 p 41.

218. *Cincinnati Enquirer.* June 13, 1937 p 61.

219. *Cincinnati Post.* June 23, 1937 p 17.

220. *Cincinnati Enquirer (Kentucky Edition).* June 16, 1938 p 12.

221. _____. November 7, 1937 p 56.

222. _____. December 16, 1939 p 21.

Chapter 3 • Xavier University

1. *The American Contractor.* Volume 31, No. 30 1910 p 51.

2. _____. Volume 31, No. 33 1910 p 44.

3. R. A. Fortin. To See Great Wonders: A History of Xavier University, 1831–006. University of Scranton Press. Scranton, Pennsylvania. 2006 p 100.

4. Sue Ann Painter. Architecture in Cincinnati: An Illustrated History of Designing and Building an American City. Ohio University Press. Athens, Ohio. 2006 p 149.

5. *Engineering and Contracting.* Volume XLIV, No. 10 1915 p 32.

6. *The American Contractor.* Volume 36, No. 23 1915 p 83.

7. *Brick and Clay Record.* July 20, 1915 p 134.

8. *The Construction Record.* Volume 53, No. 18 1915 p 12.

9. *Engineering News.* Volume LXXV 1916 p 71.

10. *The Construction Record.* Volume 34, No. 25 1916 p 1.

11. R. A. Fortin. To See Great Wonders: A History of Xavier University, 1831–2006. University of Scranton Press. Scranton, Pennsylvania. 2006 p 103.

12. The Grove Encyclopedia of American Art, Volume 1. J. M. Marter, ed. Oxford University Press. 2011 p 475.

13. R. A. Fortin. To See Great Wonders: A History of Xavier University, 1831–2006. University of Scranton Press. Scranton, Pennsylvania. 2006 p 437.

14. Cincinnati: A Guide to the Queen City and its Neighbors. City of Cincinnati, Ohio. 1943 p 314.

15. *Cincinnati Enquirer.* November 1, 1930 p 3.

16. Lee J. Bennish. Continuity and Change: Xavier University 1931–1981. Loyola University Press. Chicago, Illinois. 1981 p 117, 125–26.

17. Xavier University. Used with permission.

18. https://en.wikipedia.org/wiki/Castle_of_Xavier.

19. *The Clay Worker.* Volume LXXI, No. 6 1919 p 614.

20. *Cincinnati Enquirer.* "Real Estate and Building." April 29, 1919 p 15.

21. Photograph by J. Miles Wolf © 2020. Used with permission.

22. *The American Contractor*. Volume 43, No. 3 1922 p 76.

23. *Cincinnati Enquirer*. April 22, 1931 p 2.

24. _____. "Library Accepted by College." March 7, 1925 p 12.

25. *The Xaverian News*. "Donation of $200,000 Will Give St. Xavier Gymnasium." March 24, 1926 p 1.

26. *The Catholic Telegraph*. March 18, 1926 p 1.

27. *Cincinnati Post*. "St. Xavier will 'Step Out'." March 17, 1926 p 14.

28. *Cincinnati Enquirer*. July 18, 1926, p 4.

29. Cincinnati: A Guide to the Queen City and its Neighbors. City of Cincinnati, Ohio. 1943 p 316.

30. *Cincinnati Enquirer*. April 15, 1951 p 99.

31. _____. "St. Xavier Defeats Bearcats, 29–25, as 10,000 Look On." March 8, 1928 p 1, 16.

32. *Cincinnati Post*. September 23, 1927 p 33.

33. *Cincinnati Enquirer*. "Case No. 863-28." February 12, 1928 p 46.

34. *Xavier Magazine*. Greg Schaber, "Legends of the fall." October 2, 2004.

35. R. A. Fortin. To See Great Wonders: A History of Xavier University, 1831–2006. University of Scranton Press. Scranton, Pennsylvania. 2006 p 115.

36. *Cincinnati Enquirer*. "Denison Head to be Guest." November 18, 1929 p 21.

37. https://en.wikipedia.org/wiki/The_Best_Years_of_Our_Lives.

38. https://en.wikipedia.org/wiki/Corcoran_Stadium.

39. http://cincinnativiews.net/images-2/Xavier-z8.jpg

40. *Cincinnati Enquirer*. January 6, 1929 p 41.

41. _____. "College to Expand with Biology Building." March 5, 1929 p 3.

42. _____. April 22, 1931 p 2.

Chapter 4 • Avondale

1. D. J. Kenny. Illustrated Guide to Cincinnati and the World's Columbian Exposition. R. Clarke. 1985 p 211–213.

2. D. Stradling. *Cincinnati, From River City to Highway Metropolis.* Arcadia Publishing. Charleston, South Carolina. 2003.

3. United States Department of the Interior. National Park Service, National Register of Historic Places Registration Form. The Somerset Apartments. https://www.ohiohistory.org/File%20Library/Historic%20Preservation/National%20Register%20of%20Historic%20Places/OHSPAB/Media/Somerset_Apartments_media.pdf.

4. *Cincinnati Enquirer*. December 2, 1985 p 8.

5. Eggerding, Andrew and Clio Admin. " Cincinnati's New Orphan Asylum for Colored Youth (1845–1967)." Clio: Your Guide to History. March 24, 2018. Accessed March 25, 2021. https://theclio.com/entry/52846.

6. *Cincinnati Enquirer. (Kentucky edition).* July 4, 1947 p 4.

7. _____. November 15, 1986 p 6.

8. *The American Contractor.* Volume 40, No. 27 1919 p 78.

9. *Williams' Cincinnati Directory.* 1920.

10. Walter E. Langsam and Alice Weston. Biographical Dictionary of Cincinnati Architects, 1788–1940. Architectural Foundation of Cincinnati. Cincinnati, Ohio. 2008.

11. United States Department of the Interior. National Park Service, National Register of Historic Places Registration Form. The Somerset Apartments. `https://www.ohiohistory.org/File%20Library/Historic%20Preservation/National%20Register%20of%20Historic%20Places/OHSPAB/Media/Somerset_Apartments_media.pdf.

12. Courtesy of Hamilton County Auditor Dusty Rhodes. Parcel Number: 107-0010-0058-00.

13. *Cincinnati Enquirer.* Mark Curnutte. November 20, 2014.

14. National Register of Historic Places. http://nr.ohpo.org/.

15. National Register of Historic Places. https://www.nps.gov/nr/feature/places/14000355.htm.

16. *Saxby's Magazine.* "The Emery Estate, A Commercialized Philanthropy." Walter Maxwell. October 1909 p. 64.

17. *Cincinnati Enquirer.* November 24, 1967 p 29.

18. _____. December 21, 1999 p 4.

19. *Williams' Cincinnati Directory.* 1901.

20. _____. 1927.

21. Old Time Cinci. http://Oldtimecincy.com/.

22. Ohio Architect and Builder. "Cincinnati, Queen City of the Central West." Volume XIII, No. 6 1909 pp 24.

23. Geoffery J. Giglierano, Deborah Ann Overmyer, Frederic L. Propas. The Bicentennial Guide to Greater Cincinnati: A Portrait of Two Hundred Years. Cincinnati Historical Society. Cincinnati, Ohio. 1988 p 385.

24. National Register of Historic Places. http://nr.ohpo.org/.

25. https://www.pinterest.com/pin/380835712225487035/.

26. *The Western Architect and Builder.* Volume 21, No. 46 1904 p 2.

27. *Williams' Cincinnati Directory.* 1906.

28. *The Western Architect and Builder.* Volume 21, No. 46 1904 p 6.

29. *Ohio Architect and Builder.* "Cincinnati, Queen City of the Central West." Volume XIII, No. 6 1909 pp 9–25.

30. Saxby's Magazine. "The Emery Estate, A Commercialized Philanthropy." Walter Maxwell. October 1909 p. 62.

31. *Cincinnati Enquirer.* December 1, 1946 p 43.
32. _____. June 20, 1983 p 17.
33. Saxby's Magazine. "The Emery Estate, A Commercialized Philanthropy." Walter Maxwell. October 1909 p. 63.
34. *The Western Architect and Builder.* Volume 25, No. 6 1908 p 3.
35. *Williams' Cincinnati Directory.* 1910.
36. *Cincinnati Enquirer.* June 13, 1908 p 7.
37. *The Ohio Architect and Builder.* Volume 9, No. 1 1907 p 71.
38. _____. "Cincinnati, Queen City of the Central West." Volume 13, No. 6. 1909 p 20.
39. https://www.apartments.com/615-maple-ave-avondale-oh/teytwc9/.
40. United States Department of the Interior. National Park Service. OMB No. 1024-0018. National Register of Historic Places Registration Form. Poinciana Flats. April 21, 2014.
41. National Register of Historic Places. http://nr.ohpo.org/.
42. https://commons.wikimedia.org/wiki/File:Poinciana_Flats.jpg.
43. *Cincinnati Enquirer.* September 24, 1908 p 5.
44. _____. April 1, 1909 p 5.
45. http://www.cincinnativiews.net/apartments.htm.
46. https://www.apartments.com/624-630-rockdale-ave-cincinnati-oh/x28ry3q/.
47. *The Western Architect and Builder.* Volume 25, No. 5 1908 p 2.
48. *Engineering News.* Volume 59, No. 25 1908 p 211.
49. *The American Architect and Building News.* Volume XCIII, No. 1672 1908 p 20.
50. Courtesy of Hamilton County Auditor Dusty Rhodes. Parcel Number: 106-0003-0054-00.
51. _____. August 14, 1909 p 10.
52. *Cincinnati Enquirer.* August 21, 1909 p 9, 10.
53. _____. March 16, 1910 p 13.
54. *The American Contractor.* Volume 31, No. 15 1910 p 54.
55. *The Western Architect and Builder.* Volume 26, No. 45 1009 p 2.
56. *Cincinnati Enquirer.* February 26, 1911 p 39.
57. _____. August 5, 1923 p 54.
58. United States Department of the Interior. National Park Service. NPS Form 10-900. OMB No. 1024-0018. The Crescent. 4-30-2014 Section 8, p 10.
59. National Register of Historic Places Registration Form. http://nr.ohpo.org/.
60. *The American Contractor.* Volume 34, No. 28 1913 p 64.
61. *Cincinnati Enquirer.* July 1, 1913 p15.
62. *Cincinnati Post.* May 25, 1922 p 14.

63. *Cincinnati Enquirer.* May 25, 1922 p 8. St a
64. _____. May 3, 1925 p 66.
65. _____. September 19, 1925 p 5.
66. R. A. Fortin. Faith and Action: A History of the Catholic Archdiocese of Cincinnati, 1821–1996. Ohio State University Press. Columbus, Ohio. 2002.
67. *The Building Witness.* Volume 40, No. 35 1923 p 10.
68. *Cincinnati Enquirer.* November 9, 1935 p 25.
69. _____. December 4, 1935 (KY ed) p 24, 26.
70. _____. February 9, 1936 (KY ed) p 37.
71. *Williams' Cincinnati Directory.* 1937.
72. Courtesy of Hamilton County Auditor Dusty Rhodes. Parcel Number: 113-0004-0095-00.

Chapter 5 • Walnut Hills

1. *Architecture and Building: A Journal of Investment and Construction.* Building News Supplement. Volume 10, No. 5 1889 p 2.
2. _____. Volume 10, No. 9 1889 p 2.
3. _____. Volume 10, No. 17 1889 p 2.
4. *The American Architect and Building News.* Volume XXXVII, No. 870 1892. p xix.
5. *Cincinnati Enquirer.* February 4, 1894 p 21.
6. _____. March 31, 1894 p 16.
7. *The Inland Architect and News Record.* Volume XXIII, No. 3 1894 p 36.
8. *The Engineering Record, Building Record and Sanitary Engineer.* Volume 31, No. 4 1894 p 71.
9. M. Warminski. The Verona Apartments. National Register Information. 1998.
10. *The Ohio Architect and Builder.* "Cincinnati, Queen City of the Central West." Volume 13, No. 6. 1909 p 14.
11. Dictionary of Ohio Historic Places. Volume 1. L. K. Owen, ed. St. Clair Shores, Somerset. 1999 p 603.
12. National Register of Historic Places. http://nr.ohpo.org/.
13. Queen City Survey: Observations and Overviews of Cincinnati. Best places to experience the architecture of Joseph & Benjamin Steinkamp in Cincinnati. January 22, 2008.
14. National Register of Historic Places Registration Form. U.S. Department of the Interior, National Park Service, November 1, 2013 p 12.
15. https://www.loc.gov/resource/hhh.oh0374.photos/?sp=1.
16. *Cincinnati Enquirer.* "New life for a classic building." November 26, 2000 p 23, 28.
17. _____. "Former eyesore lauded as elegant." June 19, 2004 p 6.
18. National Register of Historic Places. http://nr.ohpo.org/.

19. Alexandria Apartment Building. http://www.cincinnativiews.net/images/Alexandria%20Apt-Walnut%20Hills.jpg.

20. *The Western Architect and Builder.* Volume 21, No. 27 1904 p 215.

21. Sanford Insurance Maps. 1904.

22. Courtesy of Hamilton County Auditor Dusty Rhodes. Parcel Number: 062-0002-0067-00.

23. Courtesy of Hamilton County Auditor Dusty Rhodes. Parcel Number: 062-0002-0063-00

24. Courtesy of Hamilton County Auditor Dusty Rhodes. Parcel Number: 062-0002-0099-00.

25. *The Ohio Architect & Builder.* Volume 3, No. 3 1904 p 55.

26. _____. Volume 3, No. 5 1904 p 54.

27. *Cincinnati Post.* April 8, 1904 p 9.

28. *The Western Architect and Builder.* Volume 21, No. 12 1904 p 6.

29. _____. Volume 21 1904 p 4.

30. *Cincinnati Enquirer.* 50 Years Ago. December 18, 1955 p 58.

31. *Ohio Architect and Builder.* Volume 6, No. 5–6 1905 p 60.

32. United States Department of the Interior. National Park Service, National Register of Historic Places Registration Form. The Somerset Apartments. https://www.ohiohistory.org/File%20Library/Historic%20Preservation/National%20Register%20of%20Historic%20Places/OHSPAB/Media/Somerset_Apartments_media.pdf

33. M. Warminski. The Verona Apartments. November 2007.

34. From the Collection of Cincinnati & Hamilton County Public Library (With permission).

35. *Cincinnati Enquirer* October 28, 1934 p 39.

36. *Cincinnati Business Courier.* March 3, 2006. https://www.bizjournals.com/cincinnati/stories/2006/03/06/story7.

37. National Register of Historic Places. 2008. http://nr.ohpo.org/.

38. Kraemer Art Co. No. 728.

39. *The American Architect and Building News.* Volume 89, No. 1575 1906 p ix.

40. *Engineering News Record.* Volume 57, No. 17 1907 p 152.

41. *Ohio Architect and Builder.* Volume 9, No. 4 1907 p 68.

42. *Western Architect and Builder.* Volume 23, No. 16 1907 p 7.

43. _____. Volume 25, No. 24 1908 p 2.

44. *Williams' Cincinnati Directory.* 1910.

45. *Western Architect and Builder.* Volume 24, No. 25 1907 p 2.

46. _____. Volume XXVI, No. 39 1909 p 2.

47. *Williams' Cincinnati Directory.* 1930.

48. *Cincinnati Enquirer.* July 22, 1909 p 13.

49. https://www.beechwoodhome.com/about/beechwood-history
50. *The Western Architect and Builder*. Volume 26, No. 32 1909 p 2.
51. Courtesy of Hamilton County Auditor Dusty Rhodes. Parcel Number: 061-0001-0017-00.
52. *Western Architect and Builder*. Volume 25, No. 20 1908 p 3
53. *Cincinnati Enquirer*. January 9, 1909 p 8.
54. _____. August 1, 1911 p 13.
55. _____. May 11, 1913 p 11.
56. *The American Israelite*. 100 Years Ago Today. September 19, 2019.
57. http://www.cincinnativiews.net/cable_cars.htm.
58. Melissa Kramer. The Inclines of Cincinnati (Images of Rail) Paperback – March 23, 2009. Arcadia Publishing p 109.
59. Walnut Hills cable railroad power house. http://jjakucyk.com/transit/carbarns/slides/0003_43727735_10215147851387278_1875726464293273600_o.html
60. Walnut Hills cable railroad power house. http://jjakucyk.com/transit/carbarns/slides/0005_Substations_Carbarns_Powerhouses-27.html
61. *Cincinnati Enquirer*. July 18, 1912 p 15.
62. _____. July 26, 1912 p 13.
63. https://digital.libraries.uc.edu/luna/servlet/view/search/what/Gilbert%2BAvenue%2B%2528Cincinnati%252C%2BOhio%2529?q=Curtis.
64. *The American Contractor*. Volume 34, No. 10 1913 p 62.
65. _____. Volume 36, No. 22 1915 p 68.
66. _____. Volume 37, No. 14 1916 p 76.
67. *Williams' Cincinnati Directory*. 1918.
68. Ursulines of Cincinnati Archives.
69. *The American Contactor*. Volume 35, No. 15 1914 p 70.
70. _____. Volume 35, No.16 1914 p 27.
71. _____. Volume 35, No. 18 1914 p 93.
72. _____. Volume 35, No. 20 1014 p 74.
73. *Cincinnati Enquirer*. April 8, 1914 p 13.
74. *The American Contractor*. Volume 38, No. 12 1917 p 62.
75. _____. Volume 38, No. 3 1917 p 68.
76. _____. Volume 38, No. 5 1917 p 79.
77. *Cincinnati Enquirer*. October 1, 1944 p 33.
78. Courtesy of Hamilton County Auditor Dusty Rhodes. Parcel Number: 067-0002-0081-00.
79. https://stfrancisds.com/wp-content/uploads/2019/03/sfds_history1.pdf.

80. _____. May 10, 1919 p 15.

81. *The Clay Worker*. Volume 72, No. 3 1919 p 233.

82. http://www.classiccarweekly.net/2013/01/02/pierce-arrow-touring-car/

83. *Engineering News Record*. Volume 86, No. 12 1921 p 164.

84. *Cincinnati Enquirer*. October 3, 1920 p 34.

85. _____. March 1, 1921 p 6.

86. *Williams' Cincinnati Directory*. 1930

87. *The American Contractor*. Volume 43. April 22, 1922 p 66.

88. _____. Volume 43. May 27, 1922 p 65–66.

89. *Cincinnati Enquirer*. February 4, 1923 p 111.

90. *The American Contractor*. Volume 43, January 14, 1922 p 67.

91. www.condokey.com/Cooper.

92. *Cincinnati Business Courier*. March 3, 2006. https://www.bizjournals.com/cincinnati/stories/2006/03/06/story7.

Chapter 6 • Clifton

1. Annual Reports of the City Departments of the City of Cincinnati for the Fiscal Year Ending December 31, 1875. Fifth Annual Report of the Clerk Office, University of Cincinnati. December 31, 1875 p 824.

2. *Cincinnati Enquirer*. March 10, 1874 p 5.

3. Kevin. Grace. Personal communication.

4. University of Cincinnati. Anonymous.

5. *Cincinnati Magazine*. "John & Katherine Kohl house." May 2006 Supp p 5.

6. _____. "On the Market: An impeccably restored Prospect Hill home." September 13, 2016.

7. WCPO News, Cincinnati. "Home Tour: Prospect Hill Queen Anne retains its original 1887 details." August 26, 2016.

8. Thomas Hadley. Personal communication.

9. C. F. Goss. Cincinnati, the Queen City, 1788–1912. S.J. Clarke Publishing Company. Chicago, Cincinnati. 1912 p 512.

10. *The American Architect and Building News*. Volume XXXVII, No. 870 1892 p xix.

11. Courtesy of Hamilton County Auditor Dusty Rhodes. Parcel Number: 102-0001-0068-00.

12. *The American Architect and Building News*. Volume LIV, No. 1093 1896 p 4.

13. United States Department of the Interior. National Park Service, National Register of Historic Places Registration Form. The Somerset Apartments. May 8, 2014.

14. Welcome to the Parkside Condominiums. http://www.theparkside.org/home.

15. National Register of Historic Places. http://nr.ohpo.org/.
16. *Cincinnati Enquirer*. July 16, 1897 p 10.
17. *Cincinnati Post*. July 16, 1897 p 4.
18. Ohio Historical Places Dictionary. Volume 2. LLC State Historical Publications. 2008 p 630–31.
19. *Cincinnati Enquirer*. Jun 21, 1984 p 44.
20. National Register of Historic Places. http://nr.ohpo.org/.
21. Queen City Survey: Best places to experience the architecture of Joseph & Benjamin Steinkamp in Cincinnati. January 22, 2008.
22. *Ohio Architect and Builder*. "Cincinnati, Queen City of the Central West." Volume XIII, No. 6
    1909 p 22.
23. *Cincinnati Enquirer*. August 4, 1957 p 74.
24. Buildings database. https://scholar.uc.edu/concern/parent/ff365c25g/file_sets/ff365c26r?locale=en.
25. S. Richards and A.S. Marks. Along Lafayette Avenue. Clifton Historic Homes: from Middleton to Mt. Storm. A Winding Publication. Cincinnati, Ohio. January 1, 2000 p 12.
26. Courtesy of Hamilton County Auditor Dusty Rhodes. Parcel Number: 218-0060-0015-00.
27. *Cincinnati Enquirer*. March 22, 1906 p 5.
28. *The Ohio Architect and Builder*. Volume 7, No. 2-6 1906 p 61.
29. National Register of Historic Places. http://nr.ohpo.org/.
30. *Cincinnati Enquirer*. "50 Years Ago Today." May 18, 1949 p 7.
31. *Cincinnati Post*. August 17, 1904 p 2.
32. *The Engineering Record*. Volume 51, No. 6 1905 p 43.
33. _____. Volume 51, No. 5 1905 p 47.
34. *The Western Architect and Builder*. Volume 21, No. 38 1904 p 4.
35. Courtesy of Hamilton County Auditor Dusty Rhodes. Parcel Number: 100-0002-0375-00.
36. *The Ohio Architect & Builder*. Volume 6, No. 5-6 1905 p 59.
37. *Cincinnati Enquirer*. June 15, 1943 p 3.
38. *The Ohio Architect & Builder*. Volume 16, No. 5-6 1905 p 59-60.
39. *Cincinnati Enquirer*. February 18, 1945 p 39.
40. *Ohio Architect and Builder*. "Cincinnati, Queen City of the CentralWest." Volume XIII, No. 6 1909 p 18.
41. *The Western Architect and Builder*. Volume 23, No. 32 1906 p 374.
42. _____. Volume 23, No. 45 1906 p 530.
43. http://www.pre-pro.com/midacore/view_distillery.php?did=DST498.

44. *The Engineering Record.* Volume 56, No. 10 1909 p 76b.
45. *Western Architect and Builder.* Volume 23, No. 19 1906 p 5.
46. _____. Volume 24, No. 13 1907 p 3.
47. _____. Volume 24, No. 12 1907 p 2.
48. *Williams' Cincinnati Directory.* 1908.
49. *Western Architect and Builder.* Volume 25, No. 14 1908 p 2.
50. *Williams' Cincinnati Directory.* 1910.
51. *The Western Architect and Builder.* Volume 25, No. 11 1908 p 3.
52. *Cincinnati Enquirer.* March 8, 1908 p 4.
53. *Williams' Cincinnati Directory.* 1910.
54. *Engineering News Record.* Volume 60, No. 2 1909 p 46.
55. *The Western Architect and Builder.* Volume 26, No. 25 1909 p 2.
56. *Cincinnati Enquirer.* August 21, 1909 p 10.
57. *The Ohio Architect and Builder.* Volume 15, No. 5 1910 p 56.
58. *The American Contractor.* Volume 31, No. 15 1910 p 54.
59. *The Western Architect and Builder.* Volume 27, No. 14 1910 p 2.
60. *The American Contractor.* Volume 35, No. 36 1914 p 77.
61. *Cincinnati Enquirer.* January 21, 1914 p 10.
62. _____. August 13, 1918 p 3.
63. *The American Contractor.* Volume 39, No. 35 1918 p 46.

Chapter 7 • Price Hill

1. Deed for 912 Suire. Hamilton County, Ohio, Harry L. Federman, Recorder. Same as #73?
2. *Williams' Cincinnati Directory.* 1928.
3. *The Western Architect and Builder.* Volume 21, No. 22 1904 p 8.
4. *Cincinnati Post.* August 17, 1904 p 2.
5. *The Engineering Record.* Volume 51. 1905 p 68.
6. Price Hill Will. https://www.pricehillwill.org/contact.
7. *Cincinnati Post.* February 22, 1905 p 8.
8. http://cincinnativiews.net/images-3/Elberon%20Apartments-Elberon%20&%20W.8th%20Sts..jpg
9. *Engineering News.* Volume LIII, No. 2 1905 p 12.
10. *The American Architect and Building News.* Volume LXXXVII, No. 1525 1905 p ix.
11. *Cincinnati Enquirer.* October 21, 1910 p 11.

12. *The Engineering Record.* Volume 59, No. 15 1909 p 42a.

13. *Cincinnati Enquirer.* September 15, 1929 p 56.

14. _____. April 18, 2012 p A1.

15. *The Western Architect and Builder.* Volume 23 1906 p 50, 65.

16. *Williams' Cincinnati Directory.* 1907.

17. Courtesy of Hamilton County Auditor Dusty Rhodes. Parcel Number: 179-0078-0193-00.

18. *The Western Architect and Builder.* Volume 23, 1906 p 482.

19. http://www.lightoverglass.com/the_lackman_building.html.

20. *Williams' Cincinnati Directory.* 1906.

21. Quadrennial Appraisement. City of Cincinnati, Ward 20. Board of Quadrennial Appraisers. Cincinnati, Ohio. 1910 p 57.

22. *Williams' Cincinnati Directory.* 1920.

23. *The Western Architect and Builder.* Volume 26, No. 16 1906 p 2.

24. *Williams' Cincinnati Directory.* 1912.

25. *The Western Architect and Builder.* Volume 23, No. 51 1906 p 593.

26. _____. Volume 23, No. 19 1906 p 221.

27. *The Ohio Architect and Builder.* Volume 10, No. 3 1907 p 53.

28. *The Western Architect and Builder.* Volume 24, No. 32 1907 p 2.

29. _____. Volume 24, No. 23 1907 p 5.

30. *Williams' Cincinnati Directory.* 1909.

31. *Cincinnati Enquirer.* February 20, 1930 p 26.

32. Ancestry.com.

33. Courtesy of Hamilton County Auditor Dusty Rhodes. Parcel Number: 179-0076-0145-00.

34. *The Ohio Architect and Builder.* Volume 10, No. 2 1907 p 54.

35. *The Western Architect and Builder.* Volume 25, No. 9 1908 p 2.

36. Saint William's Parish. Diamond Jubilee, 1984.

37. *The Western Architect and Builder.* Volume 24, No. 8 1907 p 5.

38. *Williams' Cincinnati Directory.* 1908.

39. Hamilton County Auditor. Parcel Number: 179-0078-0132-00.

40. *The Ohio Architect and Builder.* Volume 10, No. 1 1907, p 53.

41. *The Western Architect and Builder.* Volume 10, No. 3. 1907 p 2.

42. *Williams' Cincinnati Directory.* 1910.

43. *The Ohio Architect and Builder.* Volume 11, No. 3. 1908 p 61.

44. *Williams' Cincinnati Directory.* 1910.

45. *The Western Architect and Builder*. Volume 25, No. 37 1908 p 2, 5.
46. Hamilton County Auditor. Parcel Number: 177-0035-0088-00.
47. *The Western Architect and Builder*. Volume 26, No. 23 1909 p 5.
48. *Williams' Cincinnati Directory*. 1920.
49. Courtesy of Hamilton County Auditor Dusty Rhodes. Parcel Number: 180-0082-0102-00.
50. *The American Contractor*. Volume 31, No. 36 1910 p 69.
51. *The American Architect and Builder*. Volume 27, No. 36 1910 p 2.
52. _____. Volume 27, No. 18 1910 p 4.
53. _____. Volume 27, No. 41 1910 p 2.
54. *Cincinnati Enquirer*. May 3, 1928 p 24.
55. *The Western Architect and Builder*. Volume 27, No. 19 1910 p 4.
56. *Williams' Cincinnati Directory*. 1912.
57. *Cincinnati Enquirer*. April 15, 1913 p 15.
58. *The American Contractor*. Volume 34, No. 33 1913 p 72.
59. _____. Volume 39, No. 18 1918 p 70.
60. *Cincinnati Enquirer*. July 9, 1913 p 15.
61. *The American Contractor*. Volume 34, No. 28 1913 p 27.
62. _____. Volume 34. No. 33 1913 p 71.
63. *The Western Architect and Builder*. Volume 27, No. 10 1910 p 102.
64. Saint William's Parish, Diamond Jubilee. 1984.
65. *Cincinnati Enquirer*. August 24, 1912 p 7.
66. *The American Contractor*. Volume XXXVI, No. 3 1915 p 55.
67. Anne Gutzwiller. Personal communication.
68. *The American Contractor*. Volume 43, February 25, 1922 p 56
69. *Cincinnati Enquirer*. August 18, 1929 p 40.
70. _____. October 3, 1931 p 7.
71. _____. January 1, 1932 p 51.
72. *Western Architect and Builder*. Volume 26, No. 14 1909 p 3.
73. Courtesy of Hamilton County Auditor Dusty Rhodes. Parcel Number: 207-0053-0091-90.
74. *The American Contractor*. Volume 36, No. 18 1915 p 88.
75. *Williams' Cincinnati Directory*. 1916.
76. *Cincinnati Times Star*. July 15, 1970 p 13.
77. Courtesy of Hamilton County Auditor Dusty Rhodes. Parcel Number: 174-0008-0103-00.
78. *The American Contractor*. Volume 38, No. 16 1917 p 76.

79. _____. Volume 39, No. 18 1918 p 70. ETC

80. *Cincinnati Enquirer.* April 29, 1919 p 15.

81. *The American Contractor.* Volume 40, No. 10 1919 p 92.

82. Price Hill Historical Society and Museum. Used with permission.

83. *The American Contactor.* Volume 40, No. 11 1919 p 74.

84. *Cincinnati Enquirer.* August 8, 1919 p 11.

85. Price Hill Historical Society and Museum. http://www.pricehill.org/.

86. 916 Suire Deed. Hamilton County, Ohio, April 15, 1927. Harry L. Federman, Recorder.

87. *Cincinnati Enquirer (Kentucky Edition).* "Price Hill Home is 'Architectural Jewel'." May 28, 1961 p 80.

88. *Cincinnati Enquirer.* "Tudor de force." March 24, 1991 p 91.

89. *Price Hill Press.* "Couple uncovers a gem." May 9, 1990 p A1, A15.

90. *Cincinnati Enquirer.* May 27, 1928 p 51.

91. *Cincinnati Enquirer.* September 18, 1927 p 44.

92. _____. April 8, 1928 p 50.

93. _____. May 13, 1928 p 54.

94. _____. May 27, 1928 p 54.

95. _____. July 2, 1928 p 18.

96. _____. July 5, 1928 p 16.

97. _____. November 18, 1928 p 48.

98. _____. November 4, 1928 p 102.

99. _____. February 24, 1929 p 44.

100. _____. September 1, 1929 p 25.

101. _____. September 12, 1929 p 26.

102. _____. June 14, 1936 p 45.

103. *The Clay-worker.* Volume 73, 1920 p 412.

104. *Cincinnati Enquirer.* February 17, 1920 p 10.

105. *Williams' Cincinnati Directory.* 1922.

106. Courtesy of Hamilton County Auditor Dusty Rhodes. Parcel Number: 179-0077-0051-00.

107. *Cincinnati Enquirer.* October 9, 1932 p 42.

108. *Architectural Forum.* "The Five Thousand Dollar House." 1936.

109. *Cincinnati Enquirer.* September 16, 1933 p 19.

110. _____. January 21, 1934 p 33.

111. *Williams' Cincinnati Directory.* 1935.

112. Courtesy of Hamilton County Auditor Dusty Rhodes. Parcel Number: 208-0060-0092-00.

113. *Cincinnati Enquirer*. September 24, 1933 Section 2 p 1.

114. _____. November 5, 1933 p 43.

115. Courtesy of Hamilton County Auditor Dusty Rhodes. Parcel Number: 248-0001-0179-00.

116. M. Carol (Steinkamp) Molleran. Personal communication.

117. *Queen City Survey*: Observations and Overviews of Cincinnati. Joseph G. Steinkamp & Brother, Revisited. May 4, 2008.

118. https://www.realtor.com/realestateandhomes-detail/1022-Anderson-Ferry-Rd_Cincinnati_OH_45238_M44315-17626.

119. *Cincinnati Enquirer*. April 29, 1936 p 3.

120. _____. April 19, 1936 p 1.

121. _____. April 1, 1936 p 13, 15.

122. _____. December 4, 1937 p 28.

123. Phil Armstrong. Used with permission.

124. Don Juan. Lord Byron.

125. Greater Cincinnati Water Works. http://cincinnatitriplesteam.org/western_hills_station.htm.

126. *Cincinnati Enquirer*. May 29, 1936 p 20.

127. Marshall Garrison. Personal communication.

128. Cincinnati Player Piano Shop. https://www.theplayerpianoshopoh.com/.

129. Marshall Garrison. Used with permission.

130. *Cincinnati Enquirer*. April 26, 1938 p 21.

131. _____. March 19, 1938 p 19.

Chapter 8 • St. Bernard

1. *Cincinnati Enquirer*. February 11, 1892 p 12.

2. *The Ohio Architect & Builder*. Volume 6, No. 5 1905 p 63, 64.

3. *Cincinnati Enquirer*. November 30, 1905 p 5.

4. St. Bernard-Ludlow Grove Historical Society. Used with permission.

5. *The Western Architect and Builder*. Volume 23 1906 p 50.

6. *The Ohio Architect and Builder*. Volume 10, No. 1 1907 p 63.

7. *The Engineering Record*. May 2, 1891 p 361.

8. *The Western Architect and Builder*. Volume 24, No. 14 1907 p 3.

9. *Cincinnati Enquirer*. March 27, 1907 p 9.

10. *The American Contractor*. Volume 38, No. 42 1917 p 38.

11. Richard Berter. Used with permission.

12. *Fire and Water Engineering.* Volume LXV, 1919 p 1206.
13. *Cincinnati Enquirer.* May 14, 1920 p 15.
14. *The American Contractor.* June 12, 1920 p 57.
15. Marjorie N. Niesen. Images of America: St. Bernard. Arcadia Publishing. Charleston, SC. 2011 p 116. Used with permission.
16. *Cincinnati Enquirer.* February 25, 1920 p 7.
17. _____. February 11, 1929 p 2.
18. *The American Contractor.* Volume 41, No. 13 1920 p 73.
19. _____. March 1, 1921 p 6.
20. _____. May 3, 1921 p 11.
21. *WCPO News, Cincinnati.* "Wiedemann Brewing, nearly dead, to be reborn in old St. Bernard funeral home." https://www.wcpo.com/news/insider/wiedemann-brewing-nearly-dead-to-be-reborn-in-old-st-bernard-funeral-home.
22. George Wiedermann Brewing Company. Used with permission.
23. *Cincinnati Enquirer.* February 21, 1922 p 14.
24. *The Building Witness.* Volume 40, No. 5 1923 p 6.
25. Courtesy of Hamilton County Auditor Dusty Rhodes. Parcel Number: 582-0013-0131-00.

Chapter 9 • Hyde Park

1. *Cincinnati Enquirer.* September 25, 1912 p 13.
2. _____. March 19, 1913 p 10.
3. *The Ohio Architect and Builder.* Volume 10, No. 5 1907 p 62.
4. _____. Volume 9, No. 1 1907 p 71.
5. *Cincinnati Enquirer.* September 9, 1909 p 8.
6. *The American Contractor.* Volume 35, No. 14 1914 p 48.
7. *Brick and Clay Record.* Volume XLV, July-December 1914 p 293.
8. *The American Contractor.* Volume 35, No. 16 1914 p 76.
9. Cincinnati Fire Department History. http://www.cfdhistory.com/htmls/incident.php?date=2010-02-03&altime=09:37:00&name=2%20Alarm%202460%20Observatory%20Avenue.
10. *Cincinnati Enquirer.* April 9, 1914 p 15.
11. *Engineering and Contracting.* Volume 41 April 15, 1914 p 57.
12. *The American Contractor.* Volume 35, No. 16 1914 p 75.
13. *Cincinnati Enquirer.* October 14, 1914 p 12.
14. *The American Contractor.* Volume 37, No. 13 1916 p 58.

15. United States Department of the Interior. National Park Service, National Register of Historic Places Registration Form. The Almeria Flats. April 18, 2014.

16. *Cincinnati Enquirer.* August 27, 1916 p 35.

17. _____. April 15, 1923 p 43.

18. _____. December 29, 1923 p 13.

19. _____. "Many Cincinnati Families Will Greet Summer In These New Headquarters Of Happiness." February 20, 1938 p 6.

Chapter 10 • Evanston

1. *Williams' Cincinnati Directory.* 1908.

2. *The Western Architect and Builder.* Volume 21, No. 51 1904 p 5.

3. _____. Volume 21, No. 36 1904 p 4.

4. Hamilton County Auditor. Parcel Number: 057-0003-0055-00; 057-0003-0054-00; 057-0003-0053-00; 057-0003-0052-00; 057-0003-0051-00; 057-0003-0050-00.

5. *The Western Architect and Builder.* Volume 23, No. 2 1906 p 41.

6. *The Ohio Architect & Builder.* Volume 7, No. 6 1906 p 69.

7. United States Department of the Interior. National Park Service, National Register of Historic Places Registration Form. The Somerset Apartments. May 8, 2014.

8. Hamilton County Auditor. Parcel Number: 057-0003-0031-00.

9. *The American Architect and Building News.* Volume XCIV, No. 1700 1908 p 18.

10. *The Engineering Record.* Volume 58, No. 3 1908 p 50a.

11. *The Western Architect and Builder.* Volume 24, No. 45 1908 p 3.

12. _____. Volume 27, No. 16 1910 p 4.

13. Courtesy Hamilton County Auditor Dusty Rhodes. Parcel Number: 057-0003-0012-00.

14. *The Iron Trade Review.* Volume 51 1912 p 1040.

15. *The American Architect.* Volume CII, No. 1927 1927 p 14.

16. *The American Contractor.* Volume 34, No. 4 1913 p 53.

17. *Cincinnati Enquirer.* April 23, 1913 p13.

18. *Industrial World.* Volume 47, No. 1 1913 pp 609–610.

19. *Cincinnati Enquirer.* June 13, 1913 p15.

20. _____. September 29, 1936 p 5.

21. _____. January 21, 1914 p10.

22. _____. December 16, 1950 p 32.

23. www.cinematreasures.org/theaters.

24. *Cincinnati Enquirer.* July 5, 1914 p 25.

25. _____. April 8, 1914 p 13.

26. _____. August 8, 1914 p 19.

27. *The American Contractor*. Volume XXXV, No. 41 1914 p 77.

28. _____. Volume 37, No. 9 1916 p 55.

29. *Cincinnati Enquirer*. November 30, 1914 p 5.

30. _____. June 5, 1916 p 7.

31. https://abandoned.photos/post/95911328281/st-mark-catholic-church-in-cincinnati-closed.

32. *Fire and Water Engineering*. Volume 71 1922 p 695.

33. *Domestic Engineering*. Volume 99, No. 1 1922 p 349.

33. *The American Contractor*. Volume 43, No. 13 1922 p 65–66.

35. *Architectural Record*. Volume LVI, No. 3 pp 237–243.

36. _____. Volume LVI, No. 5 p 584.

37. *The Building Witness*. Volume 40, No. 7 1923 p 6.

38. *Cincinnati Enquirer*. May 20, 1933 p 23.

39. Courtesy of Hamilton County Auditor Dusty Rhodes. Parcel Number: 057-0005-0184-00.

Chapter 11 • Anderson and Mariemont

1. *Cincinnati Enquirer*. July 18, 1936 p 17.

2. _____. June 6, 1937 p 49.

3. Photograph courtesy of Nick Ganim.

4. *Cincinnati Enquirer*. October 16, 1937 p 14.

5. _____. October 14, 1945 p 41.

6. *Forest Hills Journal Press*. March 25, 1992 p 11.

7. Millard F. Rogers, Jr. John Nolen and Mariemont: Building a New Town in Ohio. Johns Hopkins Press. Baltimore, Maryland. 2001 p 124.

8. _____. p 174.

9. _____. p 175.

10. https://www.atlasobscura.com/places/chester-rows.

11. https://mariemontinn.com/historic-hotel-cincinnati/.

12. Guide to the John Dixon Johnson Architectural Drawings. 84.4.178. Newport Historical Society. Newport, RI. June 19, 2013.

Chapter 12 • Other Ohio Cities

1. *The Inland Architect and News Record*. Volume XII, No. 1 August 1888 p 9.

2. *Building (News Supplement)*. Volume IX, No. 10 1888 p 2.

3. Buildings database. https://scholar.uc.edu/concern/parent/ff365c25g/file_sets/ff365c26r?locale=en.
4. *The Western Architect and Builder*. Volume XXIII, No. 32 1906 p 374.
5. Historic Prospect Hill. http://historic-prospect-hill.org/Doron/doronshistory.pdf.
6. https://digital-collections.columbuslibrary.org/digital/collection/postcard/id/16747/.
7. *The Ohio Architect & Builder*. Volume 7, No. 5 May 1906 p 67.
8. *The Western Architect and Builder*. Volume XXIII, No. 18 1906 p 206.
9. Courtesy of Veronica Buchanan, Sisters of Charity of Cincinnati. Used with permission.
10. *The Western Architect and Builder*. Volume 23, 1906 p 518.
11. _____. Volume XXIII, 1906 p 350.
12. _____. Volume XXIII, 1906 p 182.
13. _____. Volume XXVI, No. 25 1909 p 2.
14. Walking tour of Oxford's University Historic District. p 3. http://www.cityofoxford.org/sites/default/files/comm_dev/University%20Walking%20Tour%20Brochure.pdf.
15. *The Western Architect and Builder*. Volume XXVI, No. 48 1909 p 2.
16. *The Building Witness*. Volume 40, No. 7 1923 p 6.
17. *Cincinnati Enquirer*. August 7, 1927 p 41.
18. https://www.deerparkohio.org/stjohns.htm.
19. *American Architect and Architecture*. Volume LXVIII, No. 1287 1900 p x.
20. *Cincinnati Enquirer*. January 15, 1908 p 5.
21. *The Western Architect and Builder*. Volume XXV No. 14 1908 p 2.
22. _____. Volume XXI, No. 51 1904 p 2.
23. *Williams' Cincinnati Directory*. 1906.
24. Courtesy of Hamilton County Auditor Dusty Rhodes. Parcel Number: 651-0031-0351-00.
25. *Cincinnati Enquirer*. January 21, 1914 p 10.
26. _____. March 16, 1910 p 13.
27. *The Western Architect and Builder*. Volume XXVII, No. 19 1910 p 3.
28. *The American Contractor*. Volume 34, No. 35 1913 p 65.
29. _____. Volume 35, No. 14 1914 p 95.
30. *Dayton Daily News*. November 27, 1923 p 2.
31. _____. May 18, 1930 p 21.
32. _____. January 19, 1933 p 6.
33. *The American Contractor*. Volume 35, No. 20 1914 p 74.
34. _____. Volume 35, No. 30 1914 p 16.

35. _____. Volume 35, No. 31 1914 p 36.

36. *Franklin Chronicle*. July 23, 1914 p 2.

37. Garfield Public School. Library of Congress. https://www.loc.gov/item/oh1707/.

38. *Cincinnati Enquirer*. June 9, 1925 p 12.

39. *The Ohio Architect & Builder*. Volume 10, No. 2 1907 p 51.

40. *Western Architect and Builder*. Volume XXIV, No. 27 1907 p 2.

41. Digging Cincinnati History. September 27, 2013. http://www.diggingcincinnati.com/2013/09/st-josephs-catholic-orphan-asylum.html.

42. *The Western Architect and Builder*. Volume 27, No. 16 1910 p 2.

43. *The American Contractor*. Volume 37, No. 32 1916 p 89.

44. _____. Volume 43, June 24, 1922 p 61.

45. Courtesy of Hamilton County Auditor Dusty Rhodes. Parcel Number: 196-0022-0046-00.

46. *The Western Architect and Builder*. Volume XXV, No. 17 1908 p 2.

47. *Cincinnati Enquirer*. May 10, 1919 p 15.

48. _____. September 10, 1919 p 8.

49. *The American Contractor*. Volume 40, No. 42 p 56.

50. *Cincinnati Enquirer*. July 8, 1933 p 17.

51. _____. July 21, 1933 p 19.

52. *Williams' Cincinnati Directory*. 1935.

53. _____. 1933.

54. *Cincinnati Enquirer*. March 9, 1941 p 45.

55. _____. July 25, 1941 p 19.

56. _____. May 10, 1942 p 32.

57. _____. February 9, 1907 p 10.

58. _____. April 7, 1942 p 18. 28th

59. _____. September 25, 1943 p 20.

60. Courtesy of Hamilton County Auditor Dusty Rhodes. Parcel Number: 049-0003-0258-00.

61. *Motion Picture World*. March 19, 1921 p 300.

Chapter 13 • Works out of State

1. United States Department of the Interior. National Park Service. National Register of Historic Places Inventory—Nomination Form. Emery Row. 1985. Item 8, p 2.

2. *Cincinnati Enquirer*. March 26, 1919 p 15.

3. *Cincinnati Post*. November 23, 1938 p 4.

4. *American Architect and Building News*. Volume LXXXIX, No. 1592 1906 p x.

5. *Engineering News Record.* Volume LV, No. 23 1906 p 210.

6. *Cincinnati Enquirer.* October 10, 1906 p 5.

7. *The Western Architect and Builder.* Volume 24, No. 2 1907 p 2.

8. First National Bank, Batesville, Indiana. Historical image [no date], available on Pinterest. https://images.app.goo.gl/wMZrioSijS9Ugo378.

9. *Cincinnati Enquirer.* February 25, 1910 p 13.

10. *Charleston Daily Mail.* June 7, 1931 px.

11. *The Plumber's Trade Journal.* Volume 47 1910 p 560.

12. Guide to the John Dixon Johnson Architectural Drawings. 84.4.178. Newport Historical Society. Newport, RI. June 19, 2013.

13. Realtor.com. Photograph of 386 Green End Avenue, Middletown, RI [no date]. https://www.realtor.com/realestateandhomes-detail/386-Green-End-Ave-Apt-2_Middletown_RI_02842_M42009-91698.

Chapter 14 • Patents of Joseph G. Steinkamp

1. June 2, 1903: Patent No. 729, 821: Drinking Trough for Domestic Animals. Jacob F. Weitzel. Assignor of one-half to Joseph G. Steinkamp.

2. *Cincinnati Enquirer (Kentucky Edition).* May 28, 1931 p 14.

3. September 24, 1907: US 866823: A Cabinet-kitchen. Filed October 29, 1906. Joseph G. Steinkamp.

4. *The New Yorker.* "Let's Get Small." July 25, 2011. https://www.newyorker.com/magazine/2011/07/25/lets-get-small.

5. November 5, 1929: Patent No. 1,734,748: Multi-Control Locking Mechanism. Filed August 29, 1927.

Index

Page numbers in italics refer to figures.

A

Abbotsford Apartments (132-140 W. McMillan), 84, *84*

Adkins, John Scudder, 22

The Alexandra (Taft and Gilbert Avenue), 64, 67, *68*

Alhambra building (925 Walnut Street), 31

American Beauty Home (3029 Veazey Avenue), 114–115, *115*

American Building (30 E. Central Parkway), 15, 41–43, *41–44*

American Druggists Fire Insurance Company, 41

American Institute of Architects (AIA), Cincinnati Chapter: annual convention of, 8–9; Architectural Foundation of Cincinnati and, 13; awards night of, 10–11, *11*; J. G. as active member of, 8–11

American Pharmaceutical Association (APhA), 41, 43

Anderson and Mariemont: Elstun Theater, 141; Mariemont Theater Block, 141–142, *141–142*

The Aragon, 59–60, *60*

Art Deco style, 10, 42, 95, 118

A.S. Boyle Company (1949 Dana Avenue), 137, *138*

Avery, Charles H., 43

Avondale and North Avondale: The Aragon, 59–60, *60*; The Castile, 59–60, *60*; Colored Orphan Asylum, 55, *55*, 63; The Crescent, 63, *63*–64; The Cumberland, 56, *56*; Dale home, 58; The Essex, 59, *59*; Franklin Realty Company, 64, *64*; The Granada, 59–60, *60*; Haddon Hall Apartments, 58, *58*, 64; Hale Apartments, 62–63, *63*; importance of, 55; The Madrid, *59*, 59–60; Morton garage, 64; Nicholas P. Smith & Co., 58; North and South Warwick Apartments, 56, *57*; Poinciana Flats, *61*, 61–62; St. Andrew's Parochial School, 64; The Schaffner, 60–61, *61*; Schmidt home, 64; The Somerset, 56, *57*; Streetcar Suburb Apartment Buildings, 55–56; The Virginia, 62, *62*; Waldemar Apartments, 57

B

Baas home (3645 Middleton Avenue), 91, *91*

Baas, William D., 91

Babbitt, E. J., 34

Baer, Benjamin, 157

Barlow Hodson Motor Car Company (Canal and Race Streets), 37, *37*

Barrett, Charles F., 72

Barrett home (3045 Gilbert Avenue), 72

Barrs, William E., 39

Batsche, Frank H., 69

Beal, J.H., 42, *42*

Behrens, William F., 8

Bellville apartment (751-757 Purcell Avenue), 96, *96*

Bellville, D. W., 96

Bernhardt, Jacob, 39

Berning, Joseph, 88

The Best Years of Our Lives (1946), 52

B. H. Wess Grain and Coal Company, 151

Birkmeyer, Frank, 29

Bishop, Charles E., 132

Bishop home (Perkins Lane and Stettinius Avenue), 132, *132–133*

Bismarck Café, 12, 23, *23*, 154

Boose, Joseph H., 65

Boyle, A.S., 23, 137–138

Braun, A. M., 100

Braun home (833 Suire Avenue), 100, *101*

Brew Dog Taproom, 39, *39*

Brockman, Hubert F., S.J., 50, 52

The Brookline Apartments (3401 Brookline Avenue), 90, *90*

Browning, J. C., 155

Bruce D. Robertson Design Group, 37

Burckhauser, John J., 39

Burkhardt, Joseph, 39

C

Carew, Joseph T., 72

Carter Hotel Building (Sixth and Race Streets), 32

Castellini home (1242 Edwards Avenue), 12, 129, *129*

Castellini, Joseph J., 15, 36–37, 129

The Castile, 59–60, *60*

Centennial Exposition of the Ohio Valley and Central States (1888), 1

Center Palace Hotel, 39

Central Avenue apartment, 19, *19*

Charles L. Shannon and Sons, 40

Charles Schlear Motor Car Company (Ninth and Sycamore Streets), 38, *38*

Cherdron, Daniel, 26

Cherdron home (220 E. Clifton), 26, *26*

Chevrolet Motor Car Company (2350 Gilbert Avenue), 78, *78*

The Cincinnatian, 15–16, *16*

Cincinnati Dry Cleaning Company, 63

Cincinnati Market Company market house (Sycamore Street), 36

Cincinnati's downtown. *See* downtown Cincinnati

Cincinnati Union Terminal, 10

Citizens' Bank of St. Bernard, 126, *126*

The Clermont (1404-1406 E. McMillan Street), 70, *71*

Clifton, Corryville, and Mt. Auburn: Abbotsford Apartments, 84, *84*; Baas house, 91, *91*; The Brookline Apartments, 90, *90*; Clifton Springs Distilling Company, 89, *89*; Doerr House, 90, *90*; Finn estate, 92, *92*; John and Katherine Kohl House, 81–82, *82*; Josemil Flats, 88–89, *88–89*; The Kinsey, 85, *85*, *87*; Kurz home, 82, *82*; Maplewood apartments, 85; Mayflower Apartments, 91–92, *92*; Melbourne Flats, 83, *83–84*; Parkside Apartments, 82, *83*; Pickle house, 91; Pierle house, 90–91, *91*; The Roanoke, 85, *86*; The Romaine, 85, *87*; The Roslyn, 85, *86*; The Rutland, 85–86, *87*; Siegman home, 87–88, *88*; Taft home, *84*, 85; University of Cincinnati projects, 81, *81*, 89

Clifton Springs Distilling Company (Ludlow Avenue near Mill Creek), 89, *89*

Cold storage (320 Longworth Street), 36

Cole, C. W., 85

Coleman, Fidelis, Mother, 77

Colored Orphan Asylum (Melish Avenue and Emery Avenues), 55, *55*, 63

Consolidated Trucking Company (Flint, Haefer, and Courtland Streets), 46, *46*

Cook, Louis E., 108

Cook office (3532 Warsaw Avenue), 108, *108*

Cooper Building (2324 Park Avenue), 79, *79*

Cooper, Myers Y., 51, 79

Cooper, Sanson M., 62, 79–80

Corcoran, E.B., 51

Corcoran, John, 51

Corcoran Stadium, 51–52, *52*

Cordesman-Rechtin Company (215 Butler Street), 28, *28*, 72

Corryville. *See* Clifton, Corryville, and Mt. Auburn

The Courtland Co. (725-729 Sycamore Street), 40

Courtland Flats (Sandheger flats) (117-121 E. Court Street), 21, *21*

Cracker Bakery (521 Reading Road), 26

Crane home (Mulberry Street), 31–32

Crane, Richard, 31–32, 92

Cranley, John, 58

The Crescent, *63*, 63–64

Crone, Catherine, 103

Crone home (915 Suire Avenue), 103, *103*

The Cumberland (808 Cleveland Avenue), 56, *56*

Cunningham-Holmes Company, 77

D

Dale, Ben B., 58

Dale home (Reading Road near Ridgeway Avenue), 58

Dale, Morris James, 40

Delhi. *See* Price Hill, Delhi, Westwood, and South Fairmont

designs outside Ohio: Indiana, 156; Kentucky, 155–156; Rhode Island, 157; West Virginia, 157

Devon, William P., 30

Dickman home (3542 Vittmer Avenue), 114, *114*

Dickman, J. H., 114

Dixie-Ohio Express Company (Flint and Dalton), 46

Dodge, Rose E., 141

Doerr House (3321 Morison Avenue), 90, *90*

Doerr, Walter, 90

Dorona Flats (Hamilton, OH), 145–146, *146*

Doron, Joseph W., 145–146

downtown Cincinnati: Alhambra building, 31; American Building, 15, 41–43, *41–44*; American Druggists Fire Insurance Company, 41; Barlow Hodson Motor Car Company, 37, *37*; Bismarck Café, 12, 23, *23*, 154; Carter Hotel Building, 32; Castellini home, 36; Center Palace Hotel, 39; Central Avenue apartment, 19, *19*; Charles Schlear Motor Car Company, 38, *38*; Cherdron home, 26, *26*; Cincinnati Market Company market house, 36; Consolidated Trucking Company, 46, *46*; Cordesman-Rechtin Company, 28, *28*, 72; The Courtland Co., 40; Courtland Flats, 21, *21*; Cracker Bakery, 26; Crane home, 31–32; Dixie-Ohio Express Company, 46; Duechscher home, 24–25, *25*; Emery home, 18; Ferguson apartment, 19; Fox Garage, 35, *35*; Fox Klein Motor Car Company, 39, *39*; G. H. Verkamp Clothing Store, 20, *20*; Grand Hotel, 5, 39; Greg G. Wright & Son Company, 26, *26*, 31; Harris apartment, 27, *27*; Hudepohl Brewing Company, 13, 27, 44, *45*; Imperial Hotel, 39; Kenkel Jewelry Store, 38, *38*; Kennedy Loft Building, 41, *41*; Kirchner apartments, 30, *30*; Knights of Columbus building, 40; Kroger Grocery and Baking Company, 24, 26, 27; Levinson's Furniture House, 34, *34*; Massmann home, 24, *24*; McDonald Printing Company, 29–30; Mercantile Library Building, 1–2, 15, 22–23, *22–23*, 41; Metropole Hotel, 15, 32–33, *32–33*; Norfolk Apartments, 18; Normandy Apartments, 17; Orr estate, 20, *21*; Palace Hotel, 3, 15–16, *16*, 98; Pendleton Street Apartments, 18, *18*; Pfau Manufacturing Company, 29; The Power Building, 34, *34*; Renaissance Apartments, 34; Robertson Building, 30, *31*; San Rafael Apartments, 19, *19*; The Savoy, 17, *17*; Schoolfield building, 45; Shannon garage, 40; Siefke funeral parlor, 29, *29*; Towle-Cadillac Motor Company, 36, *36*; Trum showroom, 40, *40*; Union Stock

Yards Company, 29; Waldo Apartments, 18, *18*; William Sievers Mineral Water Works, 27, *27*; William Windhorst Company, 28, *28*; Woodward Flats, 17, *17*; Young building, 45–46

Drach, Gustave, 10

Duechscher home (850 Dayton Street), 24–25, *25*

Duechscher, Max, 24

Duke Energy Convention Center, 2, 15, 17, 20

Duttenhofer, Val, Jr., 63–64

E

Eden Flats (2106 Sinton Avenue), 66, *66*

Elberon (Robertson) Apartments (3414 W. Eighth Street), 30, 97–98, *97–98*

Elet, John, 49

Elsaesser, Herman, 104

Elstun Theater (Beechmont and Plymouth Avenues), 141, *141–142*

Emery Arcade, 5

Emery Candle Works, 124, *124*

Emery Estate, 22, 32

Emery flat (2220 Gilbert Avenue), 65, *65*

Emery home (301 W. Fourth), 18

Emery House (Covington, KY), 155, *155*

The Emery House (Covington, KY), 155

Emery, J. Howard, 2

Emery, John J., Sr., 2, 18, 55

Emery, Mary, 3, 31, 143

Emery Row Apartments (2152-2156 Gilbert Avenue), 66, *66*

Emery, Thomas J., 2, 55. *See also* Thomas Emery's Sons

Emery, Thomas L., 2

The Essex (Reading Road and Cleveland Avenue), 59, *59*

Evanston: A.S. Boyle Company, 137, *138*; Evanston Theater, 138, *138*; Frey home, 140; Fritsch and Hugle homes, 148, *148*; LaSalle Apartments, 135, *135*; Pachoud garage, 137, *137*; Richter home, 137; St. Mark's Catholic Church, 138–139, *139*; St. Mark's Parochial School, 140, *140*; Sister's Home, St. Marks' Church, 136; Smith home, 140, *140*; Strothman home, *136*, 137

Evanston Theater, 138, *138*

F

Farrin, M. B., 151

Felsberg, Nelson, 1, 6, 10, 13, 44, 46, 114–117, 120–121, 132

Feltes, George H., 104, 109

Feltes home (861 Academy Avenue), 104, *104*

Ferguson apartment (Dayton Street and Freeman Avenue), 19

Ferguson, Edward A., Hon., 19

Finn estate (Vine and Charlton Streets), 92, *92*

First National Bank (Batesville, IN), 156, *156*

Forbeck, John, 104

Forn, Catherine, 103

Fox, Frank, 35

Fox Garage, 35, *35*

Fox Hardware Store and Flat (2436 Gilbert Avenue), 75, *76*

Fox Klein Motor Car Company (316 Reading Road), 39, *39*

Fox, Mary, 75

Frank, J.O., 64

Franklin Hotel Company, 149

Franklin Realty Company (Burnet and Northern Avenues), 64, *64*

Frazer, J.C., 141

Freericks, Frank H., 41, 43

French Benzol Dry Cleaning Company (Florence Avenue and Concord Street), 74, *74–75*

Frey, Albert, 140

Frey home (Woodburn and Gilpin Avenues), 140

Fritsch and Hugle homes (Norwood, OH), 148, *148*

Fritsch, Joseph, 136, 148

F. & W. Siefke, 29, *29*

G

Garfield Public School (South Cummingsville, OH), 150, *150*

The Garonne (2663 Gilbert Avenue), 77, *77*

Garrison home (2855 Urwiler Avenue), 120, *120–121*

Garrison, James Harwood, 120

G. C. Riordan Studio, 107

George Wiedemann Brewing Company, 126, *127*

Georgian Terrace Apartments (2136 Madison Road), 61, 130, *131*

G. H. Verkamp Clothing Store (312 W. Fifth Street), 20, *20*

Gilbert Avenue Cable House, 74, *75*

Gillespie, Cecil Howard, 1, 6, 10, 13, 44, 46, 114–117, 120–121, 132

Government and Fountain Squares (proposed, 1915), 35, *35*

Graeter, Richard, 82

The Granada, 59–60, *60*

Grand Hotel, 5, 39

Greg G. Wright & Son Company, 26, *26*, 31

Grunkermeyer, Edward, 124

Guaranty Realty Company, 72

H

Haberer, E. J., 149

Hackman, G. L., 147

Haddon Hall Apartments (3814 Reading Road), 58, *58*, 64

Hake, Harry, 10, 34, 37, 78

Hale Apartments (576 Hale Avenue), 62–63, *63*

Hall home (3445 Observatory Place), 132, *132*

Hall, John H., 132

Hannaford, Samuel, 2, 15, 18, 72, 81

Harris apartment (128 Findlay Street), 27, *27*

Harris, George R., 27

Hartman, E. H., 102

Hazard home (3816 W. Eighth Street), 96

Hazard, Minnie, 96

Hellenschmidt, Julius, 104, 110

Hellman, Johanna, 117

Henry Imwalle Funeral Parlor, 124, *124*

Henthorn, Henry E., 1

Herbert, Jeffrey, 3

Hillenbrand & Company, 156

Himpler, Francis G., 77

Hinkle, Frederick W. (Susanna), 48

H.L. Stevens & Co., 33

Holz, Fred, 90

Home for Incurables, 73, *73*

Hotel Metropole (609 Walnut Street), 15, 32–33, *32–33*

Hudepohl Brewing Company, 13, 27, 44, *45*

Hudepohl, Louis, 21

Hugle, William, 148

Hulbert Taft House (439 Lafayette Avenue), *84*, 85

Hurtt, Francis, 24

Hyde Park: Bishop home, 132, *132–133*; Castellini home, 12, 129, *129*; Georgian Terrace Apartments, 61, 130, *131*; Hall home, 132, *132*; Schaffner home, 130, *131*; Siefke home, 129, *130*

I

Imperial Hotel, 39

Imwalle, Frank, 126

Imwalle, Henry, 124

Imwalle Memorial (4811 Vine Street), 126, *126–127*
Imwalle Undertaker Company, 126
Indiana designs, 156

J

John and Katherine Kohl House (519 Liberty Street), 81–82, *82*
Josemil Flats, 88–89, *88–89*
Joseph G. Steinkamp and Bro, Architects and Superintendents. *See also specific designs, neighborhoods, and people*: AIA and, 8; building code modifications and, 8, 51, 64, 121, 141; formation of, 1; offices of, 1–2; overview of, 1–3; stylistic approach of, 56, 61, 66–67, 83, 85, 95, 106, 118, 147, 150

K

Kaiser home (1234 Ross Avenue), 95
Kaiser, William A., 95
Kalling, William, 82
Kealy, Joseph, 98
Kenkel, Henry, 146
Kenkel Jewelry Store (1302 Main Street), 38, *38*
Kennedy Loft Building (118 E. Eighth Street), 41, *41*
Kennedy, Thomas E., 34, 41
Kenny, Daniel J., 55
Kentucky designs, 155–156
Kerl, Emma, 117
Kerl/Hellman duplex (2934 Harrison Avenue), 117, *117*
Kinker, Frank, 18
The Kinsey (2415 Maplewood Avenue), 85, *85*
Kirchner apartments (221 W. Ninth), 30, *30*
Kirchner, Frank, 30
Knights of Columbus building (14-18 E. Ninth Street), 40
Kramer, Anton, 149

Kroger bakery (Newport, KY), 155, *156*
Kroger, B. H., 24, 151
Kroger Grocery and Baking Company, 24, 26, *27*, 155
Krug Realty Company, 62
Krushing, J.B., 81
Kuhlman, G., 17
Kurz, Fred, 82
Kurz home (3202 Glendora Street), 82, *82*

L

Lackman, Henry F., 98
Laidlaw, Robert, 92
Langsam, Walter, 67
LaSalle Apartments (3501 Montgomery Road), 135, *135*
Leibold-Farrell Construction Company, 52
Lester, Florence, 114
Lester home (4534 Lower River Road), 114
Levinson's Furniture House (313 W. Fifth Street), 34, *34*
Lippelman, J. H., 20
Little Sisters of the Poor Home for the Aged (Montgomery Road opposite Symmes), 66
Livingood, Charles, 141
L.S. Murdock Printing Company, 30

M

The Madrid, *59*, 59–60
Maplewood Apartments, (3440 Telford Street), 85, *87*
Mariemont (Middletown, RI), 157, *157*
Mariemont Theater Block, 141–142, *141–142*
Mason Towle Company Dodge (2230 Gilbert Avenue), 78, *78*
Massmann home (1320 Penddleton Street), 24, *24*
Matthews, Stanley, 43
Maxwell, Walter, 58

Mayflower Apartments (3201 Vine Street), 91–92, *92*
McDonald, Andrew J., 30
McDonald Printing Company, 29–30
McLellan, Mary Carmel, 77
McMicken Health Collaborative, 44
McNicholas, John T., 107
Melbourne Flats (39 W. McMillan Street), 83, *83–84*
Menke apartment (3961 W. Eighth Street), 99, *100*
Menke home (905 Suire Avenue), 100, *100*
Menke, Loius, 99–100
Mercantile Library Building (414 Walnut Street), 1–2, 15, 22–23, *22–23*, 41
Merrill Corporation of Chicago (Northside, OH), 151
Metropole Hotel, 15, 32–33, *32–33*
Meyer, Frank A., 128
Meyer home (3265 Vittmer Avenue), 114, *114*
Meyer home (4253 Bertus Street), 128, *128*
Meyer, Peter, 114
Meyer, Richard, 114
Miami University, 147
Middendorf home (822 Rosemont Avenue), 109
Middendorf, Joseph, 109
Milk Money (1994), 82
Miners, H. E., 145
Moeller, William, 77, 105, 107, 139
Montifer, E., 102
Moore, Alexandra, 67
Moorman Avenue homes (2554-2560 Moorman Avenue), 68, *69*
Morton, C. P., 64
Morton garage (3864 Reading Road), 64
Mt. Auburn. *See* Clifton, Corryville, and Mt. Auburn
Mueller, Max, 149
Murdock Printing Company, 30
Murry, John B., 139

N

Nagle, Henry, 121
Nagle home (3410 Hazelwood Avenue), 121, *121*
Nau, Louis J., 64
The Navarre (Gilbert across from Yale Avenue), 70, *70*, 77
Nelson Apartments (McMillan Street and Kemper Lane), 67, *67*, 72
Nicholas P. Smith & Co. (3437 Wilson Avenue), 58
Nicolai, Adam, 121
Niedenthal, Andrew, 138
Norfolk Apartments, 18
Normandy Apartments (Race and Longworth Streets), 17
North and South Warwick Apartments (Blair Avenue and Reading Road), 56, *57*
North Avondale. *See* Avondale and North Avondale
Northside Distilling Company, 40
Nurre duplex (4343 Errun Lane), 127, *128*
Nurre, H., 123
Nurre house (171 Church Street), 123, *123*
Nurre, Joseph, 127

O

Oakley apartment (28th Street and Robertson Road), 154
Oberhelman, John, 102
O'Brien, Robert J., 52
Ohio designs outside Cincinnati. *See* other Ohio cities
Ohio Electrolytic Oxygen Company, 34
Ohio National Guard Armory, 40
Ohio State Association of Architects, 8
Old St. Mary's Church, 3, *3*, 5, *5*

Order of Alhambra, 31
Orr estate (24 W. Court Street), 20, *21*
Oskamp home (2440 Harrison Avenue), 108, *108*
Oskamp, William S. P., 30
Oskamp, W. W., 108
Osthoff home (459 Purcell Avenue), 98–99, *99*
Osthoff, John B., 98
Ostholthoff and Braukman carriage plant, 34
Ostholthoff, Henry, 34
other Ohio cities: Cheviot, 146; Cummingsville and South Cummingsville, 150; Dayton, 149; Deer Park, 148; Fayetteville, 146; Franklin, 149; Hamilton, 145–146; Hartwell, 145; Lima, 147; Lockland, 151–152; Milford, 146; Northside, 151; Norwood, 148–149; Oakley, 154; Oxford, 147; Pleasant Ridge, 152; Toledo, 145; Winton Place, 151; Wyoming, 149
Our Lady of Mercy Church, 149

P

Pachoud, A. L., 68, 135, 137
Pachoud garage (3410-3421 Montgomery Road), 137, *137*
Paddack, Alice and Mary, 98
Paddock home (525 Rosemont Avenue), 98, *98*
Palace Hotel, 3, 15–16, *16*, 98
Parkside Apartments (3315-3317 Jefferson Avenue), 82, *83*
patents of Joseph G. Steinkamp, 159–161
Peabody Homestead, 69
Pendleton Street Apartments, 18, *18*
Perrin Estate, 21
Peters, William, 91
Pfau Manufacturing Company (Spring and Twelfth Streets), 29
Pickel, Peter, 91
Pickle home (310 Goodman Street), 91
Pierce-Arrow cars, 77, *78*
Pierle, Charles E., 90
Pierle home (3439 Middleton Avenue), 90–91, *91*
Pilder's Food Market, 64
Pitton Brothers, *83*
Planet Dance, 78, *79*
Plaza Hotel, 39
Poetker, Henry, 14, 20
Poinciana Flats (3522 Reading Road), *61*, 61–62
The Power Building (Kennedy Power Building) (337 Main Street), 34, *34*
Price Hill, Delhi, Westwood, and South Fairmont: American Beauty Home, 114–115, *115*; Bellville apartment, 96, *96*; Braun home, 100, *101*; Cook office, 108, *108*; Crone home, 103, *103*; Dickman home, 114, *114*; Elberon Apartments, 30, 97–98, *97–98*; Feltes home, 104, *104*; Garrison home, 120, *120–121*; Hazard home, 96; Kaiser home, 95; Kerl/Hellman duplex, 117, *117*; Lester home, 114; Menke apartment, 99, *100*; Menke home, 100, *100*; Meyer home, 114, *114*; Middendorf home, 109; Nagle home, 121, *121*; Oskamp home, 108, *108*; Osthoff home, 98–99, *99*; Paddock home, 98, *98*; Price Hill Historical Society, 104, 110, *110*; Price Hill Knights of Columbus, 109, *109*; Provident Savings Bank and Trust Company, 109–110; Schell home, 109; Schwartz home, 113, *113*; Siefke home, 115, *116*; Stein home, 102, *102*; Treinen home, 116, *116*; U.S. Electric Tool Company, 104, 109, *109*; Vonderahe home, 99, *99*; Vonderhaar home, 102–103, *103*; Western Hills Pumping Station, 118–119, *118–119*; Westwood First Presbyterian Church, 120, *120*; Zugelter home, 101, *101*
Price Hill Historical Society (3640 Warsaw Avenue), 104, 110, *110*

Price Hill Knights of Columbus (Fairbanks Avenue), 109, *109*

Provident Savings Bank and Trust Company (3640 Warsaw Avenue), 109–110

Provident Savings Bank and Trust Company (Northside, OH), 151, *151*

Q

Queen City Club, 5

R

Ransley Apartments, 72

Reardon, Francis, 107

Rechtin home (1725 E. McMillian Street), 72, *73*

Rechtin, Louis E., 28, 72, *73*

Red Fox Grill, 45, *45*

Reeve home (2223 Fulton Avenue), 79

Reeve, J. H., 79

Renaissance Apartments (224 E. Eighth Street), 34

Rhode Island designs, 157

Richter home (3528 Wabash Avenue), 137

Richter, Marie, 137

The Roanoke (359 Ludlow Avenue), 85, *86*

Robertson Building (Race and Seventh Street), 30, *31*

Robertson, Musco M., 30, 97

Robertson Realty, 97

Rockne, Knute, 51

Roessler, A.D., 152

Roessler home (Pleasant Ridge, OH), 152, *153*

Rogers, Millard, 142

The Romaine (3421 Middleton Avenue), 85, *87*

Roos, A. E., 76

Roos, Henry, 76

Roos home (Lincoln Avenue near Winslow Street), 76

The Roslyn (3404-3420 Middleton Avenue), 85, *86*

Roth, Francis, Rev., 104, 106, 121

Roth, George F., 11

The Rutland (358 Shiloh Street), 85–86, *87*

S

St. Aloysius Academy (Fayetteville, OH), 146, *146*

St. Andrew's Parochial School (Blair Avenue and Reading Road), 64

St. Bernard: Citizens' Bank of St. Bernard, 126, *126*; Emery Candle Works, 124, *124*; George Wiedemann Brewing Company, 126, *127*; Henry Imwalle Funeral Parlor, 124, *124*; Imwalle Memorial, 126, *126–127*; Meyer home, 128, *128*; Nurre duplex, 127, *128*; Nurre house, 123, *123*; St. Bernard Fire House, 125, *125*; St. Bernard Town (City) Hall, 125, *125*; St. Clement's School, 124

St. Bernard Fire House, 125, *125*

St. Bernard Town (City) Hall, 125, *125*

St. Clement's School, 124

St. Francis De Sales Church parish house (Woodburn and Madison Roads), 77

St. John's School (Deer Park, OH), *148*, 148–149

St. Joseph's Orphan Asylum (Norwood, OH), 148, 150

St. Louis Flats, 58, 88, 100

St. Mark's Catholic Church (3500 Montgomery Road), 138–139, *139*

St. Mark's Parochial School, 140, *140*

St. Mary's Catholic Church, 149

St. Rita School for the Deaf, 151

St. Ursula Academy, 76, *76*

St. William Catholic Church: addition on, 106–107, *107*; Men's Society of, 104; Parish House of, *106*; photos of, *105*, *107*; School of, 105, *105–106*; style of, 106

Samuel Hannaford and Sons, 40

Sandheger, Christopher, 21
San Rafael Apartments (Fourth Street), 19, *19*
The Savoy (225 W. Court Street), 17, *17*
Sawyer, Frank, 77
Sawyer home (McMillan and Stanton Avenues), 77
The Schaffner (615 Maple Avenue), 60–61, *61*
Schaffner, Clarence E., 60–61, 130
Schaffner home (2460 Observatory Avenue), 130, *131*
Schell, Charles, 109
Schell home (1021 Del Monte Place), 109
Schlacks, H.J., 138
Schmid, George, 50
Schmidt, Charles, 64
Schmidt home (Erkenbrecher and Vine Street), 64
Schmidt, Walter S., 50
Schoolfield building (209-211 E. Third Street), 45
Schoolfield, Georgianna, 45–46
Schwartz, Edward, 113
Schwartz home (4519 Glenway Avenue), 113, *113*
Seifke family, 29
Seton Realty Company, 93
Shannon, Charles L., 40
The Shannon Company, 40
Shannon garage (17 E. Canal Street), 40
Shaw, A. A., 51
Siefke, Ed, 29, 129
Siefke funeral parlor (Eighth and Linn streets), 29, *29*
Siefke home (1011 Anderson Ferry Road), 115, *116*
Siefke home (Observator and Michigan Avenues), 129, *130*
Siefke, Martha Menke, 115
Siefke, William G., 129

Siegman, Anthony, 87
Siegman home (2367 Rohs Street), 87–88, *88*
Sieve, Clifford B., 112
Sister's Home, St. Marks' Church (Montgomery Pike and Duck Creek Road), 136
Sisters of Charity, 146, 148
Siter, Henry, 150
Smith, Edward J., 140
Smith home (2003 Crane Avenue), 140, *140*
Smith, Nicholas P., 58, 63
The Somerset (Reading Road and Blair Avenue), 56, *57*
South Fairmont. *See* Price Hill, Delhi, Westwood, and South Fairmont
S. S. Kresge Company, 7–8
Stein home (810 Pedretti Avenue), 102, *102*
Stein, Joseph C., 102
Steinkamp, Anna, 14
Steinkamp, Bernard. *See also* Joseph G. Steinkamp and Bro, Architects and Superintendents: birth of, 11; death of, 12; early designs of, 12; education of, 11; family of, 11; homes of, 136, *136*, 152, *153*; lack of writing on, 12; marriage of, 11; overview of, 11–13; photos of, *12*; professional career of, 13
Steinkamp, Cecelia, 14
Steinkamp, Clara, 136
Steinkamp, Elizabeth, 14
Steinkamp, George J., 6, 13–14, *14*
Steinkamp home (916 Suire Avenue) (J. G.), 95, *95*, 110–112, *110–112*
Steinkamp home (1022 Anderson Ferry Road) (J. G.), 115, *115*
Steinkamp home (1931 Clarion Avenue) (Bernard), 136, *136*
Steinkamp, Johan Herman Heinrich, 3
Steinkamp, Johann Bernard (J. B.): birth of, 3; death of, 1; early designs of, 5; education of, 4; family of, 4; first

projects of, 4, 81; marriage of, 4; offices of, 1, 4; overview of, 3–5; photos of, *4*; several names of, 3–4

Steinkamp, Joseph G. *See also* Joseph G. Steinkamp and Bro, Architects and Superintendents: birth of, 5; building code work of, 8–9; death of, 6; early career of, 15; education of, 5; family of, 6; golden pocket watch gift of, *5*, 5–6; homes of, 6, 95, 99, 110–112, 115; lack of writing on, 6–7; legal career of, 9–10; marriage of, 5; offices of, 1, 22; overview of, 5–11; patents of, 159–161; personal life of, 7–8; photos of, *5*, *9*; professional life of, 8–11

Steinkamp, Katherine (Catherine), 14

Steinkamp, Laura (Menke), 5, 7, 104

Steinkamp, Maria Elizabet (Kramer), 3

Steinkamp, Mark, 13

Steinkamp, Mary Elizabeth (Ahrens), 4–5

Steinkamp, Robert G., 13

Steinkamp, Robert J., 13

Steinkamp, Rose, 14

Sterling Glass Company, 23, *23*

Storer, Bellamy, 76

Storer, Maria Longworth, 76

Stradling, D., 55

Strange, Victor, 78

Strashun, A., 60

Strauss, Joseph, 81

Strauss, Morris, 63

Streetcar Suburb Apartment Buildings, 55–56

Strothman, Charles, 137

Strothman home (3610 Bevis Avenue), *136*, 137

Suire, Hannah A., 95

Suire, Marion L., 110

Sullivan home (1387 Myrtle Street), 73–74, *74*

Sullivan, M. J., 73

T

Taft home (439 Lafayette Avenue), *84*, 85

Taft, Hulbert, Sr., 85

Talbot Apartments, 18

Tallawanda Apartments (Oxford, OH), 147, *147*

Tapke, Herman, 17

Telford and Groesbeck, 27

Thien, H. B., 150

Thien home (Cummingsville, OH), 150

Thomas E. Kennedy & Company, 32

Thomas Emery's Sons: Avondale and, 55–56, 58–59, 63; Clifton and, 82, 85; downtown Cincinnati and, 17, 19, 32; overview of, 1–2; Walnut Hills and, 65–67, 70, 77; work outside of Ohio and, 145, 156

Thoms, Joseph C., 32–33

Towle-Cadillac Motor Company (1120 Jackson Street), 36, *36*

Treinen home (5024 Cleves-Warsaw Pike), 116, *116*

Treinen, Ray, 116

Trum, August B., 40

Trum showroom (922 Race Street), 40, *40*

U

Union Stock Yards Company, 29

University of Cincinnati, 3–4, 81, *81*, 89

U.S. Electric Tool Company, 104

U.S. Electric Tool Company (2490 River Road), 104, 109, *109*

V

Verkamp, G. H., 20

The Verona (2356 Park Avenue), 64, 71, *71*–72

The Virginia (624-630 Rockdale Avenue), 62, *62*

Vonderahe, Anna G., 99

Vonderahe home (816 Suire Avenue), 99, *99*

Vonderhaar, Henry, 102
Vonderhaar home (2504 Homestead Place), 102–103, *103*

W

Wahl, John, 146
Waldemar Apartments (Reading Road and Hickman Avenue), 57
Waldo Apartments (Eighth and Elm Streets), 18, *18*
Walnut Hills and East Walnut Hills: The Alexandra, 64, 67, *68*; Barrett home, 72; Chevrolet Motor Car Company, 78, *78*; The Clermont, 70, *71*; Cooper Building, 79, *79*; Cunningham-Holmes Company, 77; Eden Flats, 66, *66*; Emery flat, 65, *65*; Emery Row Apartments, 66, *66*; Fox Hardware Store and Flat, 75, *76*, *76*; French Benzol Dry Cleaning Company, 74, *74–75*; The Garonne, 77, *77*; Gilbert Avenue Cable House, 74, *74–75*; The Goronne, 77, *77*; Harrison home, 77; Home for Incurables, 73, *73*; Klein street homes, 65; Little Sisters of the Poor Home for the Aged, 66; Mason Towle Company Dodge, 78, *78*; McMillan Street and Kemper Lane apartments, 72, *72*; The Navarre, 70, *70*, 77; Nelson Apartments, 67, *67*, 72; Rechtin home, 72, *73*; Reeve home, 79; Roos home, 76; St. Francis De Sales Church parish house, 77; St. Ursula Academy, 76, *76*; Sawyer home, 77; Sullivan home, 73–74, *74*; The Verona, 64, 71, *71–72*; Worchester home, 77
Warminski, M., 70
Washington, Booker T., 55
Wefler Grounds baseball park (Oakley Park, OH), 12, 154
Weitzel, Jacob F., 159
Western Hills Pumping Station (1650 Queen City Avenue), 118–119, *118–119*
West Virginia designs, 157
Westwood. *See* Price Hill, Delhi, Westwood, and South Fairmont
Westwood First Presbyterian Church (3011 Harrison Avenue), 120, *120*
W.F. Beherns & Company, 23
William Sievers Mineral Water Works, 27, *27*
William Windhorst Company (1201 Main Street), 28, *28*
Wilson, Russell, 141
Woodward Flats (64 Woodward Street), 17, *17*
Wray-Chase Motor Service Company, 36

X

Xavier University: Albers Hall, 47, 52, *53*; Alumni Science Hall, 49; beginning of collaboration, 47; building codes and, 51; Corcoran Stadium, 51–52, *52*; Edgecliff Hall, 47, 49, *49*; Elet Hall, 47, 49, *49*; Field House, 47; Football Stadium, 47, *51*; funding raising for, 47, 50; Gymnasium, 47, 50–51; Hinkle Hall, 47–48, *48*; importance of, 47; Schmidt Hall, 47, 50, *50*; stylistic elements of, 47, 51–52; Union Building, 47

Y

Young building (213-219 E. Third Street), 45–46
Young, H. H., 45–46
Young Men's Mercantile Library Building (414 Walnut Street), 1–2, 15, 22–23, *22–23*, 41

Z

Zugelter, H. H., 101
Zugelter home (945 Sunset Avenue), 101, *101*

Acknowledgments

First of all, I must thank my dear wife, Janet, for allowing me to hijack the spare bedroom for a couple of years when my book outgrew the small office downstairs.

Many people helped me in different ways to obtain all the information for this book. It all started with my realtor, Ellen Epstein, when she showed me Joseph's home in Price Hill.

Two individuals were instrumental in piquing my interest in Joseph Steinkamp after I purchased his home. Mike Maio and his late wife, Janet Kearns, had done some research into the Steinkamps before I purchased the home from them, and they shared that information with me. When I came across a couple of blogs in which Susan Lee, a great granddaughter of Joseph, summarized some of the brothers' works, I decided to dig into their history a little deeper.

Seleen Collins was invaluable as a writer/editor in reviewing what I had written and especially in editing the hundreds of references in the book.

Sandra "Mickey" deVise, Reference Librarian of the Cincinnati History Library and Archives, Cincinnati History Museum, was invaluable in helping me locate many of the buildings that the Steinkamps designed and providing guidance on researching Cincinnati's past.

Joyce Meyer of the Price Hill Historical Society provided a great deal of information about the many buildings in Price Hill designed by the brothers.

Nancy Broermann, Archivist, St. Ursula Academy, provided both information about the work the Steinkamps did for Maria Longworth Storer at St. Ursula Academy and inspiration after she published her own book on Maria.

Anne Ryckbost, University Archivist and Special Collection Librarian, Xavier University Library, allowed me to search the Xavier files and provided me with several early photos of the Xavier campus.

Dave Pittinger of the Hamilton County Recorder's Office and Paula Drake of the County Auditor's office were invaluable in locating many of the buildings designed by the Steinkamps.

Dusty Rhodes, Hamilton County Auditor, kindly provided several photos of buildings that were no longer standing as well as photos that were difficult to obtain.

Klaus Steinkamp, a distant relative in Germany, provided information about the early history of the Steinkamp family.

Jill Beitz, Manager, Reference and Research, Cincinnati History Library and Archives, Cincinnati Museum Center, helped locate photos in the collection.

A number of descendants of Joseph and Bernard provided valuable information about the family. Dr. Stephen Steinkamp, the late M. Carol (Steinkamp) Molleran, Bill Molleran, Susan Lee, and Bernard Steinkamp were especially helpful.

Geoff Sutton of the Walnut Hills Historical Society provided information about the work of the Steinkamps in Walnut Hills, along with photos of some of their buildings.

Betty Ann Smiddy, a local historian and author, was helpful in sorting out some of the details about buildings designed by the brothers.

Marge Niesen, President of the St. Bernard–Ludlow Grove Historical Society, provided photos of the brothers' works in St. Bernard.

Kay Phillips, of the St. Bernard–Ludlow Grove Historical Society, was a valuable resource for uncovering information about the Steinkamps' work in St. Bernard.

Several other individuals provided useful information and/or photographs for the book:

- Valda Moore, Price Hill Historical Society, and husband, Robert, owners of Joseph's home at 912 Suire Avenue
- Tom and Peggy Rice
- Veronica Buchanan, Archivist, Sisters of Charity of Cincinnati, Seton Hall, Mount St. Joseph
- John Zimkus, Warren County Historical Society's Harmon Museum
- Susan Scouras, The Culture Center, Charleston, WV
- Anne Senefeld, Digging Cincinnati History
- Anne Delano Steinert, OTR Museum/University of Cincinnati
- Kevin Grace, Archives & Rare Books Library and University Archivist, University of Cincinnati
- Chris Smith, Reference Librarian, Cincinnati Public Library
- J. Miles Wolf
- D. Weise
- Phil Armstrong
- George Verkamp
- Greg Terhune
- Marshall Garrison

About the author

Thomas (Tom) H. Connor, PhD

Tom lives in Price Hill in the home Joseph Steinkamp designed as his own with his wife, Janet, Miley their dog, and several cats. Tom was a member of the faculty of the University of Texas School of Public Health in Houston for twenty years and a researcher at the National Institute for Occupational Safety and Health in Cincinnati for another twenty. His work won him numerous awards and he has traveled the world to present his research at scientific meetings. He has authored about one hundred scientific and government publications, but this is his first endeavor at writing a book.